SAN FRANCISCO
TRIVIA

SAN FRANCISCO TRIVIA

TRIVIA

BILL DOLON & KAREN WARNER

101 PRODUCTIONS
SAN FRANCISCO

COVER PHOTO: Rik Olson
COVER DESIGN: Lynne O'Neil
COVER ACKNOWLEDGMENTS: Kaufer-Stadler Company, San Francisco,
Mission Dolores model; Jim Kelly, Pat O'Shea's Mad Hatter, Super Bowl Tickets; King's
Baseball Cards, Berkeley, Willie Mays card; Charlotte Mailliard, official key to The City;
Leon Numainville, Zap Comics first editions; Bruce Taylor, Mystery Book Shop,
Maltese Falcon.

Published by 101 Productions, 834 Mission Street,
San Francisco, California 94103.
Distributed to the book trade by
The Scribner Book Companies, New York.

Library of Congress Cataloging-in-Publication Data
Dolon, Bill.
    San Francisco trivia.

    Includes index.
    1. San Francisco (Calif.)—Miscellanea.   2. Questions
and answers.   I. Warner, Karen.   II. Title.
F869.S345D65   1985   979.4'61   85-15383
ISBN 0-89286-255-6

TO MIKE — THE RISK WAS ALL ON YOU.——K.W.
FOR LARRIE.——B.D.

A special thank you to the staff of 101 Productions,
our agents Michael Larsen and Elizabeth Pomada,
and Robert Barrett, the consummate native.

So many people went out of their way to help us with this project
that we feel the book is as much theirs as it is ours. Here is a list,
by no means complete, of the people to whom we wish to express
our heartfelt gratitude.

Roy Allinson, Simpson College
Eugene Andersen, San Francisco Fire Department
Andy Anderson, Southern Pacific Railroad
Lynn Atwood, University of California
Patricia Barich, Lowry and Partners
Nikki Bengal, *San Francisco Chronicle*
Liz Black, Golden Grain Macaroni Company
Marvin Boyd, El Cid
Lynn Brown, Mark Hopkins Hotel
Jeannie Candau, San Francisco Museum of Modern Art
Michele Canning, National Conference of Christians and Jews
Chris Chiarrella, Four Seasons Clift Hotel
Peg Clark
Inez Cohen, San Francisco Public Library
Mike and Danny Conroy
Melanie Daly, St. Francis Hotel
Ernie Domecus, City College of San Francisco
Ann Dingwall, Oceanic Society
Betsy Dixon, San Francisco Symphony
Teddy Eggleston, Caltrans
Ellen Elias, San Francisco Ballet
Carl English, San Francisco Fire Department
Susan Fahey, Maud's
Virginia Felker, Alameda Naval Air Station
David Fleishhacker, Katherine Burke School
Charles Foll
John Gettys, San Francisco Public Library
Debbie Hale, The Sharper Image
Jesse Hamlin, *San Francisco Chronicle*
Gladys Hansen, San Francisco Public Library
Mary Haverstock, Ghirardelli Square
Nancy Hayden, Lowry and Partners
Fred and Phyllis Henwood, Little Hollywood Improvement Club
Bill Hillman, KPIX
Mary Ann Hogan, *Oakland Tribune*

Rita Hughes, KTZO
Mike Iapoce, Golden Gate Writers
Duffy Jennings, San Francisco Giants
Ernestine Jones, Stanford University
Denise Joseph, George Washington High School
Julie Kavanagh, Visitation Valley Community Center
Kevin Keating, *San Francisco Chronicle*
Jim Kelly, *San Francisco Progress*
Ross Kleinschmidt, Cable Car Museum
Karl Kortum, San Francisco Maritime Museum
Les Krames, KRON
Marvin Lewis
Lou Lillian, San Francisco Board of Supervisors
Joan Lynn, Golden Grain Macaroni Company
Harry Mara, San Francisco State University
William McCoy, San Francisco Bay Bombers
Julia McHugh, Lucasfilms
Ken McNeil, Treasure Island Naval Station
Bob Mitchell, KGO
Louise Molinari, God Squad Productions
J. B. Murphy, St. Ignatius College Preparatory School
Leonard Nelson, KNBR
Frank Norrell, Little Hollywood Improvement Club
Hector Novarro
Hadley Osborn, Filoli Foundation
J. P. O'Shea, *San Francisco Chronicle*
Shelley Paxson, University of San Francisco
Karolyn Raush, Kolmar/Raush
Kevin Reneau, University of California
Al Rossi, Podesta Baldocchi
Juanita Rusev
Jacquie Sartain
Jan Simmons, Bill Graham Productions
Peter Simon, University of San Francisco
Tony Stratta, San Francisco Italian Athletic Club
Mary Ann Tabor, Belli and Associates
Clifford Uyeda, M. D., Japanese American Citizens League
Gloria Valentine, Hoover Institution
Judy Van Austen, Oakland Coliseum
Patty Wada, Japanese American Citizens League
Garry Wommack, San Francisco Police Department
Anita Wood, Golden State Warriors
Robert Yanagi, San Francisco Forty Niners

CONTENTS

MY FAVORITE SAN FRANCISCO TRIVIA

AL ATTLES
GOLDEN STATE WARRIORS

Q. Who was the Warriors' opponent when Al Attles won his five-hundredth NBA game as head coach?

A. The Dallas Mavericks.

ENRICO BANDUCCI,
VIOLINIST AND RESTAURATEUR.

Q. What famous San Francisco cabaret almost was named the Song Cellar?

A. Some people were opening up a place across the street from the hungry i. They were going to put pictures of singers on the walls and call it the Song Cellar. I said, "My God, what a terrible name! Even Purple Onion is better than that." And that's what it became.

MELVIN BELLI
ATTORNEY AND GIANTS FAN

Q. On January 24, 1962, the *Chronicle* front-page headline read: "Giants Lose, 11–1." Who won?

A. When the Giants moved to Candlestick, their ticket brochure specifically promised "radiant heating." After almost freezing my backbone off, I sued for a refund. My expert witnesses were Marines from an arctic survival unit who testified that the ballpark was colder than the icecap. The jury voted 11–1, in my favor.

VIDA BLUE
SAN FRANCISCO GIANTS

Q. On April 17, 1979, the Oakland A's had their smallest crowd in the Coliseum's history with 653 people. Can you name these people?

ERSKINE AND SHIRLEY BUFANO
THE BUFANO SOCIETY

Q. Which of the following statements about Beniamino Bufano are true?
    a) He designed the buffalo on the buffalo nickel.
    b) He cut off his right index finger and sent it to Woodrow Wilson to protest World War I.
    c) He gave Franklin D. Roosevelt the idea to wear a cape.

A. All of the statements are true.

PERRY BUTLER
RESTAURATEUR AND OWNER OF PERRY'S

Q. What New York City bar was the inspiration for Perry's?

A. Most people think it was P. J. Clarke's, but actually most of my feelings and ideas that went into Perry's came from Martell's on Eighty-third and Third.

JOHN CANTU
COMEDY IMPRESARIO

Q. How did the Holy City Zoo comedy club get its name?

A. The Holy City's zoo, in the Santa Cruz mountains, had gone bankrupt and the owner of the comedy club bought the zoo's tables and chairs at auction. Included in his purchases was the sign to the Holy City Zoo which the owner hung outside the comedy club.

JOE CARCIONE
THE GREEN GROCER

Q. Mark Twain referred to what vegetable as the "cabbage with a college education"?

A. Cauliflower.

DWIGHT CLARK
SAN FRANCISCO FORTY NINERS

Q. The San Francisco Forty Niners' Super Bowl roster listed two players who did not play collegiate football. Instead they were world-class track and field performers. Can you name them?

A. Wide receiver Renaldo Nehemiah and nose tackle Jeff Stover.

VINCENT DeDOMENICO, PRESIDENT
GOLDEN GRAIN MACARONI COMPANY
MAKERS OF RICE-A-RONI

Q. Rice-A-Roni, the "San Francisco Treat," is actually what Old World recipe?

A. Middle Eastern pilaf. It's made with long-grain rice, thin vermicelli and chicken broth.

STRANGE DE JIM

Q. Why is Herb Caen called "Bubbles"?

A. Some say it is because of his habit of eating Mexican food and then soaking in a hot tub with a bottle of champagne.

STANTON DELAPLANE
COLUMNIST, SAN FRANCISCO CHRONICLE

Q. What was San Francisco's Prosperity Corner?

A. Prosperity Corner was a street corner not far from Cookie Picetti's Star Cafe, where, it was alleged, the now departed McDonough brothers used to pay off the cops in the 1930s.

FRANK DILL AND MIKE CLEARY
KNBR RADIO PERSONALITIES

Q. Who is Madame Illya Dillya?

A. Comedienne Phyllis Diller. After gaining national attention as a performer at San Francisco's Purple Onion, Phyllis appeared as a piano soloist with symphony orchestras across the country. Using the name Illya Dillya, she performed with the San Francisco Symphony in June, 1972.

JIM EASON
COMMUNICASTER, KGO RADIO

Q. The original Spanish name for Twin Peaks, *Los Pechos de la Choca*, translates to mean what?

A. The Breasts of the Indian Maiden.

LAWRENCE FERLINGHETTI
POET AND PUBLISHER, CITY LIGHTS BOOKSTORE

Q. How did City Lights Bookstore get its name?

A. McCarthyism was prevalant when Peter Martin and I opened the bookstore in 1953. We named it after the film of Chaplin, whose Little Man has always been a symbol of the subjective man, a free individual against the authoritarian world.

JACK FERTIG, A.K.A. SISTER BOOM BOOM
NUN OF THE ABOVE

Q. Where was the Sisters of Perpetual Indulgence founded?

A. Iowa City, Iowa, on Holy Saturday, 1979.

PHIL FRANK
TRAVELS WITH FARLEY

Q. Name the San Francisco hill where a flock of thirty wild parrots make their home.

A. Telegraph Hill. The birds are escapees from private individuals.

ANN FRASER AND ROSS McGOWAN
PEOPLE ARE TALKING, KPIX-TV

Q. Name the famous cowboy who is buried in Colma.

A. Wyatt Earp.

PETE GIDDINGS
KGO-TV METEOROLOGIST

Q. How many microclimates are there in the City of San Francisco?

A. Based on temperature, fog and wind, there are basically five microclimates in the city. 1) The Fog Belt (Sunset, Lake Merced, Richmond, Seacliff and the Presidio); 2) Pacific Heights, the Marina, Cow Hollow and North Beach; 3) the area east of Twin Peaks or the Banana Belt (Mission and Potrero Hill); 4) Bay View and Hunters Point and 5) the downtown area.

MARK GORDON
THE GREAT SAN FRANCISCO TRIVIA GAME

Q. As a child during the 1906 earthquake, he broke his nose and his doctor advised him to have it fixed when he grew up. He never had it fixed because he claimed he never grew up. Who was he?

A. Ansel Adams.

BILL GRAHAM
ROCK IMPRESARIO

Q. Name the three acts that performed the first show at Winterland on September 23, 1966.

A. Paul Butterfield Blues Band, Jefferson Airplane and Muddy Waters.

JERRY GRAHAM
BAY AREA BACKROADS, KRON-TV

Q. In the original Broadway production of *I Remember Mama*, which is set on Steiner Street in San Francisco, who played the character Niles?

A. Marlon Brando.

BILL GRIFFITH
ZIPPY THE PINHEAD

Q. Due to its tapered top, the Transamerica Pyramid is known by employees by what nickname?

A. The Zippy the Pinhead Building.

MICHAEL HEATON
PM, SAN FRANCISCO EXAMINER

Q. Where did Al Jolson die and what was he doing when he died?

A. Al Jolson was playing gin rummy with his manager at the St. Francis Hotel when he died.

KRAZY GEORGE
BAY AREA CHEERLEADER

Q. In what year did Pele play against the San Jose Earthquakes soccer team?

A. August, 1975.

FRED LaCOSSE AND TERRY LOWRY
AM SAN FRANCISCO, KGO-TV

Q. Who was the voice of C. Dudley Nightshade on the *Crusader Rabbit* television show?

A. Russ Coughlin.

THE HONORABLE HARRY W. LOW
PRESIDING JUSTICE, DISTRICT FIVE
STATE COURT OF APPEAL, FIRST APPELLATE DISTRICT

Q. Name the ex-San Francisco supervisor who tried to emulate Charles Crocker by using Chinese workers successfully to build a railroad across Chile, Peru and Argentina.

A. Henry Meiggs, who left San Francisco after stealing $300,000 in city funds and twenty-three volumes of records. Meiggs eventually paid back all the money with interest, but the governor refused to cancel the arrest warrant. In South America, where he died, he is considered a hero.

CYRIL MAGNIN
CHIEF OF PROTOCOL FOR THE CITY AND
COUNTY OF SAN FRANCISCO

Q. After the 1906 earthquake the Fire Department didn't have enough water to fight the fires. Name the street that was dynamited on both sides to create a fire block in order to control the blaze.

A. Van Ness Avenue.

CHARLOTTE MAILLIARD
DEPUTY CHIEF OF PROTOCOL FOR THE CITY OF SAN FRANCISCO

Q. In what two cities did Mayor Dianne Feinstein break her arm?

A. Xian, China, and Washington, D.C.

PAT McCORMICK
DIALING FOR DOLLARS, KTVU-TV

Q. Who was the host of the *Captain Satellite* kiddie show and what is he doing now?

A. Bob March. He left the popular television show in the 1970s and is now a therapist and family counselor.

R. C. OWENS
SAN FRANCISCO FORTY NINERS

Q. Name the former Forty Niner who was a number-one draft choice and the only man to replace Ted Williams of the Boston Red Sox as a pinch hitter.

A. Carroll Hardy.

TOM PARKER
KFRC RADIO PERSONALITY

Q. Before Joe DiMaggio was married to Marilyn Monroe, he was wed to another Hollywood actress. Who was she?

A. Dorothy Arnold.

CARL PAYNE, DING DONG DADDY
CABLE CAR BELL-RINGING CHAMPION

Q. How do the cable car conductor and gripman communicate?

A. By means of a bell-ringing code: One ring to stop, two to start, three for emergencies and four when it's safe to back up.

DAVEY ROSENBERG
TOPLESS DANCING'S CREATOR

Q. Name the topless dancer who chained herself to the Golden Gate Bridge in 1965 to protest attempts to deport her to Persia.

A. Yvonne D'Angers.

MAL SHARP
MAN-IN-THE-STREET INTERVIEWER

Q. Name the North Beach club that featured the world's first and only all-girl-topless band.

A. Tipsy's.

STEVE SILVER
BEACH BLANKET BABYLON

Q. Who was the rock group that was refused the key to the City of San Francisco when they made their final concert performance at Candlestick Park in 1966?

A. The Beatles.

JEREMIAH TOWER
OWNER/CHEF, STARS AND THE SANTA FE BAR & GRILL

Q. This nobleman was the manager of the Palace Hotel in the 1940s.

A. Baron Edmond A. Rieder, from 1942 to 1957.

JOAN WESTON
BAY BOMBERS

Q. The San Francisco Forty Niners are the oldest sports franchise in the Bay Area. Can you name the second-oldest franchise?

A. The Bay Bombers formed in 1954 and the Forty Niners in 1946.

SAN
FRANCISCO
TRIVIA

PEOPLE & LIFESTYLES

MONDO BIZARRO
Welcome to Kook City

1   Who was the candidate in the 1980 Board of Supervisors race called the "pastrami candidate"?

2   Two mongrel dogs became so famous in the 1860s that when one of them died, ten thousand people attended his funeral and Mark Twain wrote his eulogy. Name the dogs.

3   In 1964, a jury awarded a woman victim of a cable car accident $50,000. She claimed the mishap caused this condition.

4   This Bay Area school offers a two-credit course in chocolate.

5   In 1979, her T-shirt said "Pardon me" on the front and "Being kidnapped means always having to say you're sorry" on the back.

6   Who was Sergeant Sunshine?

7   In 1979, this man was fired from the *San Francisco Examiner* after it was discovered that he had written an "eyewitness account" of a journey to China without having gone there.

8   What was Gayle Spiegelman's unusual title when she danced at the North Beach club El Cid in 1968?

9   In the early 1970s, this bar's men's room had a magnifying glass above the urinals and showed movies of dancing go-go girls at eye level.

10   Name the group that had a midnight show in 1970 at the Palace Theatre called "Tinsel Tarts in a Hot Coma."

MONDO BIZARRO
Welcome to Kook City

1   Carl La Fong ran on a platform of better delicatessen food. He supported an ordinance to ban the playing of disco music within five hundred feet of any living thing, and, if elected, promised to bring the seriousness to the Board of Supervisors that it deserved by wearing a rabbit suit to every meeting. He finished thirty-fourth out of sixty-five candidates for eleven seats.

2   Bummer and Lazarus. When Bummer died, he was eulogized by Twain. When Lazarus died, he was stuffed and put on display.

3   She claimed the accident had made her a nymphomaniac.

4   U.C. Berkeley. It is a two-credit course taught by the faculty of the Botany Department.

5   Patricia Hearst.

6   San Francisco Police Sergeant Richard Burgess. In 1967, Burgess, a twelve-year veteran, smoked marijuana on the steps of the Hall of Justice to protest dope laws. He was accompanied by a crowd of hippies jingling tambourines and tossing posies. He was arrested and served six months in San Bruno Jail.

7   Bob Patterson.

8   Topless Mother of Eight. She was, too.

9   Ripples, now Barnaby's, in Embarcadero One.

10 The Cockettes. This group's persona fell somewhere between a hippie commune and the Radio Music Hall Rockettes. Some of their names were Goldy Glitter, Hibiscus and Dusty Dawn.

AMAZING EFFECTS OF FOG ON THE TONGUE
Local Quotables

1   This man claimed the coldest winter he ever endured was a summer in San Francisco.

2   Who said: "I'm what might be called a reform candidate. I want to keep Sausalito from going off half-cocked."?

3   When this incumbent supervisor was re-elected in 1979 he exclaimed: "It's humbling that all this energy came together around me. I'm in an abnormal state of consciousness right now."

4   While visiting The City, this famous husband and wife acting team remarked: "Lynn and I would like nothing better than to settle down to live here—except of course that we already live in Wisconsin."

5   In 1959, a nationally famous comedian was questioned by police after trying to climb the rigging of the *Balclutha* at Fisherman's Wharf. "Where I from? I'm from outer space, man, outer space. I'm the man in the moon. I'm John Q. What's it to you?" Who is John Q?

6   He called San Francisco "The Cool Grey City of Love."

7   Who said, "I always see about six scuffles a night when I come to San Francisco. That's one of the town's charms."?

8   In 1965, when this entertainer fell out of his second-story hotel room window, his obscene tirade so upset the hospital medics that they taped his mouth shut. Who was he?

9   In 1985 who remarked: "Premature ejaculations by committee members are frankly not at all helpful."?

10   He said: "Make no mistake, stranger, San Francisco is West as all Hell."

AMAZING EFFECTS OF FOG ON THE TONGUE
Local Quotables

1   Mark Twain.

2   Former madam Sally Stanford, while running for Sausalito City Council in 1962.

3   Supervisor Harry Britt, after defeating Terence Hallinan in a runoff. This was his first victory at the polls, after being appointed to the board.

4   Alfred Lunt and Lynn Fontanne.

5   Jonathan Winters was taken from the *Balclutha* to San Francisco General for observation, but not before he said: "This boat is a fake. It's got an outboard motor on it." Winters later admitted to nervous exhaustion and apologized.

6   Poet George Sterling.

7   Errol Flynn. It seems the handsome actor was a swashbuckler both on and off the screen.

8   Lenny Bruce. He claimed he was standing on the window sill explaining freedom to a friend, when he accidentally fell.

9   Mayor Dianne Feinstein. She was exasperated with unauthorized news leaks to the press by the Baseball Stadium Task Force.

10   Poet Bernard DeVoto.

GREAT PLACES TO BE FROM
Birthplaces of Famous San Franciscans

1   This supervisor and former candidate for mayor was born in Syracuse, New York.

2   Where was Enrico Banducci born?
    a) Palermo, Italy.   b) Oakland.   c) Bakersfield.
    d) New York's Little Italy.

3   Joe DiMaggio grew up in North Beach. Where was he born?

4   Which of the following people were born in Texas?
    a) Willie Brown.   b) Harry Britt.   c) Charlotte Mailliard.

5   Where was singer/restaurateur Boz Scaggs born?

6   How many of The City's thirty-seven mayors were not born in San Francisco?
    a) 10.   b) 15.   c) 28.   d) 31.

7   This Ukrainian-born violinist made his concert debut with the San Francisco Symphony at age eleven.

8   This attorney, the epitome of a big-city lawyer, was born in Sonora.

9   Where is Forty Niners owner Eddie DeBartolo, Jr. from?

10   Born in San Francisco, he is noted for his poems about Chicago and New England.

GREAT PLACES TO BE FROM
Birthplaces of Famous San Franciscans

1 Quentin Kopp. Seven of The City's mayors were born in New York State.

2 Bakersfield.

3 Martinez, California.

4 All of them. Willie Brown is from Mineola, Harry Britt was born in Port Arthur and Charlotte Mailliard hails from Kilgore.

5 Canton, Ohio.

6 Twenty-eight. San Francisco's nine native mayors are Levi Ellert, James Phelan, Eugene Schmitz, James Rolph Jr., Elmer Robinson, John Shelley, Joseph Alioto, George Moscone and Dianne Feinstein. A non-native has not been elected mayor since 1955.

7 Isaac Stern, who was brought to San Francisco when he was a year old and later graduated from the San Francisco Conservatory of Music. When New York's Carnegie Hall was scheduled for demolition in 1960, Stern was primarily responsible for saving it.

8 Melvin Belli.

9 Youngstown, Ohio. As a matter of fact, he still lives in Youngstown.

10 Robert Frost.

CLOSE BUT NO CIGAR
Rodney Dangerfield Awards

1 This man actually conceived the idea of having a "street railroad propelled by an underground endless rope" around 1870. Unable to finance its construction, he sold the entire project to Andrew Hallidie.

2 On November 16, 1542, this famous Portuguese explorer discovered the Farallon Islands but couldn't find San Francisco Bay.

3 This man found the first nugget of the Gold Rush, and lost it. His claim was jumped, and he later died in abject poverty.

4 Name the man who missed becoming San Francisco's first official resident by twelve months and five days.

5 On August 2, 1873, he came within seconds of being the world's first cable car operator. Then what happened?

6 This civil engineer designed a transcontinental railroad over the Sierra Nevada mountains. But when he died in 1863, the Big Four had already forced him out of any profits.

7 St. Francis of Assisi is The City's patron saint. Name another St. Francis who has a church named after him in San Francisco.

8 Who was San Francisco's second mayor?

9 Name the backup quarterback for Joe Montana in Super Bowl XVI.

10 Who was the winner of the 1976 San Francisco Comedy Competition when Robin Williams came in second?

CLOSE BUT NO CIGAR
Rodney Dangerfield Awards

1   Benjamin H. Brooks.

2   Juan Rodriguez Cabrillo. History records him as the discoverer of San Diego Bay and Alta California.

3   James Marshall.

4   Jacob P. Leese built the second house in Yerba Buena Cove, next to the residence of Captain William A. Richardson. This makes Leese San Francisco's official first neighbor?

5   Plain and simple, he looked down the hill and chickened out. Then he jumped off the cable car and into obscurity. History leaves us with one word of physical description: pale.

6   Theodore D. Judah. Instead of having a hotel, bank or university named after him, he got an avenue out in the Sunset.

7   St. Francis Xavier at Octavia near Pine.

8   Charles James Brenham.

9   Steve Deberg. (Did you guess Guy Benjamin?)

10   Bill Farley. Sometimes second place isn't so bad.

I'LL NEVER FORGET OLD WHATSIZNAME
Nicknames and Aliases

1   Born Mabel Janice Busby, she was a San Francisco madam, then a restaurateur and a politician.

2   On Alcatraz, this Chicago mobster was prisoner #85.

3   The Symbionese Liberation Army named her Tania.

4   Who is Wolfgang Grajonca?

5   Jack Rosenberg came to San Francisco and built an empire of self-actualization seminars using his new name. What is it?

6   Snooky is the nickname of this former police chief and supervisor.

7   This *San Francisco Chronicle* pop music and film critic was listed in the local phone directory as Joaquin Bandersnatch.

8   Grimes Polnikov is one of San Francisco's tourist attractions. By what name is he more commonly known?

9   On October 28, 1936, Cardinal Eugenio Pacelli blessed the recently completed Bay Bridge. By what title was he later known?

10 In 1949, a San Francisco federal court convicted Iva Toguri of treason for making English broadcasts for the Japanese during World War II. What did the newspapers call her?

I'LL NEVER FORGET OLD WHATSIZNAME
Nicknames and Aliases

1   Sally Stanford. Miss Stanford was known by a variety of names, stemming from her six marriages as well as a long list of police bookings. Testifying before a liquor control board hearing in 1955, she said she could not remember when she adopted the name Sally Stanford, but she could recall that Stanford defeated California in the annual Big Game that year.

2   Al Capone.

3   Patty Hearst. After being kidnapped by the SLA she was named after Tania Burke, a guerrilla killed while fighting alongside Che Guevara in Bolivia.

4   Rock impresario Bill Graham.

5   Werner Erhard, founder of est.

6   Al Nelder.

7   John Wasserman.

8   The Human Jukebox.

9   Pope Pius XII.

10   Tokyo Rose. It was later proven that there were at least thirteen other "Tokyo Roses," yet only Miss Toguri was charged. It was also revealed that Iva smuggled food and medicine to American POWs at grave personal risk. This revelation led to her public support and in 1977 President Gerald Ford granted her an unconditional pardon.

THE GOOD, THE BAD AND THE UGLY
San Francisco Personalities

1   He was instrumental in bringing the King Tut exhibit to San Francisco in 1979.

2   Daughter of an Oakland jazz musician, she went on tour with Prince in 1984.

3   What deed put Douglass Cross and George Cory in San Francisco's heart?

4   Name the author who worked writing advertising copy for Samuels Jewelers on Market Street.

5   This Barbary Coast character would let you hit him with a bat for a fifty-cent piece.

6   Born in San Francisco, she helped revolutionize dancing in the twentieth century.

7   Name the artist who created the controversial bust of George Moscone.

8   Carol Channing graduated from this San Francisco high school.

9   Her book *The Intruders* tells of living in a haunted house on Lombard Street.

10   This former political candidate is employed at the Jewish Community Center handing out towels.

THE GOOD, THE BAD AND THE UGLY
San Francisco Personalities

1   Cyril Magnin, chief of protocol for the City of San Francisco. Magnin traveled to Cairo and invited Sadat to close the exhibition in San Francisco at the end of the American tour.

2   Sheila E (Escovedo).

3   Cross wrote the lyrics to "I Left My Heart in San Francisco"; Cory, the music.

4   Dashiell Hammett.

5   Oofty Goofty.

6   Isadora Duncan. As a child, growing up in San Francisco, she taught dancing to neighborhood children.

7   Robert Arneson. The Moscone bust, which included a pedestal containing graffiti and bullet holes, was promptly removed from Moscone Center after its unveiling.

8   Lowell High School. At an early age, Channing opted for a show-business career, while seated on her grandmother's lap to see Ethel Waters in *As Thousands Cheer* at the Curran Theatre.

9   Pat Montandon.

10 Sister Boom-Boom (Jack Fertig).

THE GOOD, THE BAD AND THE UGLY RETURN
San Francisco Personalities II

1   This local journalist published his autobiography, *If You've Got a Lemon, Make Lemonade*, at age twenty-nine.

2   Every time he wins a major legal case, this San Francisco attorney fires off a cannon and hoists the Jolly Roger above his office.

3   He founded the hungry i and Enrico's.

4   Anyone who has ever heard Norbert Yancey improvise calypso songs remembers his music. At what corner is he always found performing on weekends?

5   Name the nationally famous mime who honed his skills by mimicking people that walked through Union Square.

6   In 1947, this woman founded and let the Citizen's Committee to Save the Cable Cars in a successful campaign against City Hall action to replace the cable cars with diesel buses.

7   To many San Franciscans, twin sisters Vivian and Marian Brown are as much city landmarks as the spires of Sts. Peter and Paul. What is their unique distinction?

8   They were married at City Hall on January 15, 1954.

9   In 1985, this man won the cable car bell-ringing contest for the seventh time in nine years.

10 What do Steven Spielberg, Placido Domingo, Willie Nelson, Henry Winkler and Peter Morton have in common?

THE GOOD, THE BAD AND THE UGLY RETURN
San Francisco Personalities II

1   Warren Hinckle.

2   Melvin Belli.

3   Enrico Banducci.

4   Beach and Larkin. Besides his calypso tunes, he also performs folk songs in fifteen languages and is an operatic tenor, a martial arts instructor and a TV stuntman.

5   Robert Shields.

6   Friedel Klussmann.

7   They always do everything together and they dress identically.

8   Joe DiMaggio and Marilyn Monroe.

9   Muni gripman Carl Payne.

10   They are all part owners of the Hard Rock Cafe.

COUNTER CULTURES

1   In July of 1976, six young men in Paul Revere costumes, complete
     with three-cornered hats and buckled shoes, appeared at
     Fisherman's Wharf. They were carrying a supply of carnations and
     Back to Godhead magazines. Who were they?

2   The Ancient Order of E Clampus Vitus was founded in Sierra City,
     California, in 1857. By what name are they better known?

3   This militant group forced a recall election of Mayor Dianne
     Feinstein in 1983.

4   According to statistics compiled by Werner Erhard and Associates,
     how many San Franciscans have taken est training?
     a) 1 in 364.   b) 1 in 105.   c) 1 in 69.   d) 1 in 94.

5   What is COYOTE?

6   In 1983, this group tore down the Confederate flag from the
     display of historical flags in front of City Hall to protest racism.

7   This organization, founded by Maggie Kuhn, strives to protect the
     rights of the elderly.

8   Their symbol was the seven-headed cobra.

9   This coffeehouse in North Beach was the central gathering place
     for the 1950s Beat Generation.

10   Prior to moving to the South American jungle, this group's
     headquarters was located at 1859 Geary Street, near Fillmore.

COUNTER CULTURES

1 Devotees of the International Society for Krishna Consciousness. One devotee explained the radical departure from their traditional saffron-robed, shaved-head look: "We have to preach to the time, the place and circumstances, and this is the Bicentennial Year."

2 The Clampers. Founded with a purpose of poking fun at other fraternal organizations, their highest club officer is called the Grand Noble Humbug.

3 The White Panthers. Their efforts to have Mayor Feinstein recalled were unsuccessful.

4 One in 69.

5 COYOTE is the organization devoted to improving the lot of the prostitute. COYOTE stands for Call Off Your Old Tired Ethics.

6 The Spartacist League.

7 Gray Panthers.

8 The Symbionese Liberation Army.

9 The Co-Existence Bagel Shop.

10 The Peoples Temple.

FAMOUS ALUMNI

1   This temple of higher learning granted a college degree to Beaver Cleaver.

2   Herbert Hoover was a member of this school's first freshman class in 1891.

3   Where did O. J. Simpson attend college before he transferred to USC?

4   Famous for his expertise in the field of semantics, this former president of San Francisco State became a California senator in 1976.

5   Albert Michelson was America's first Nobel laureate. Where did he attend high school?

6   Bobby Seale and Huey Newton met as classmates in 1966 at the old Grove Street campus of Merritt College. What organization did they found together?

7   Lana Turner briefly attended this high school in the Avenues.

8   In 1978, the mayor, the speaker of the state assembly, and the governor were all graduates of this San Francisco high school.

9   While at Lowell High School, this famous California politician acquired his nickname by imitating Patrick Henry.

10 His master's thesis at San Jose State was titled "Defensing the Pro Spread."

FAMOUS ALUMNI

1   Gerald (Jerry) Mathers, U.C. Berkeley, Class of '74. Prior to becoming an Old Blue, Mr. Mathers was the star of *Leave it to Beaver*.

2   Stanford.

3   City College of San Francisco.

4   Republican Senator S. I. Hayakawa (1976–80).

5   Albert Michelson graduated from Lowell High School in 1868 and won the Nobel Prize for physics in 1907.

6   The Black Panthers.

7   Washington High School.

8   St. Ignatius Preparatory. Its graduates were George Moscone, Leo McCarthy and Jerry Brown.

9   Former California Governor Edmond G. "Pat" Brown.

10   Bill Walsh, Forty Niners head coach.

THE GAY LIFE

1   According to a market research study conducted in 1984, how many gay men live in San Francisco?

2   What was Harvey Milk's occupation before he entered politics?

3   Name The City's gay men's dance hall that opened, briefly, in 1908.

4   This is San Francisco's only exclusively gay bookstore.

5   In 1971, this militant group was founded by Reverend Ray Broshears, to counter a rash of anti-gay street violence.

6   Name the Polk Street shop whose marquee offers daily homilies like "Eat, Drink and Be Mary" and "Sex is Nobody's Business but the Three People Doing It."

7   This was the first gay bar in The City to have open picture windows.

8   What is the name of San Francisco's gay-owned banking institution?

9   This is the oldest gay Democratic club in San Francisco.

10 Name the oldest women's bar in The City.

THE GAY LIFE

1   In 1984, a city-financed professional study by Research and
     Decisions Corporation determined that The City's gay male
     population was 70,000. It also estimated that 44 percent of them
     earned more than $25,000 annually, and two-thirds were under
     the age of 39.

2   Camera shop owner on Castro Street.

3   The Dash. Originally it had dancing girls, but new owners replaced
     them with men. City Hall political infighting is credited with its
     demise.

4   Walt Whitman Books on Market Street.

5   The Pink Panthers.

6   Sukkers Likkers.

7   The Twin Peaks, at Castro and Market.

8   Atlas Savings and Loan.

9   The Alice B. Toklas Memorial Democratic Club, founded in 1971.

10   Maud's at 937 Cole opened in 1964.

MONEY MAKES THE WORLD GO 'ROUND
The Rich

1   Founded by A. P. Giannini, this bank was first called Bank of Italy.

2   Who is the richest man in the San Francisco Bay Area?
       a) William Randolph Hearst, Jr. b) David Packard.
       c) Gordon Getty. d) Robert Lurie. e) William Hewlett.

3   Founder of the Bank of California, in 1869 he robbed the U.S. Subtreasury of a million dollars. He was never punished for the crime.

4   The Board of Supervisors voted to have him relocate his Sutter Street clothing store, when it was learned he had withheld rent money from the city.

5   What Civil War general once operated a bank on the corner of Jackson and Montgomery?

6   Under his leadership, the *San Francisco Examiner* had the first comic strip and the first foreign correspondent.

7   Which is taller: the Transamerica Pyramid or the Bank of America World Headquarters?

8   Name the singer who starred in a series of black tie optional concerts at Oakland's Paramount Theatre in 1974.

9   How did Nob Hill get its name?

10   After this mayor (1902–07) was convicted of twenty-seven counts of graft and bribery and sentenced to fourteen years in San Quentin, San Franciscans elected him to the Board of Supervisors. Who was the mayor?

MONEY MAKES THE WORLD GO 'ROUND
The Rich

1   Bank of America, founded in 1904.

2   If you guessed Gordon Getty, you're wrong. *Forbes* magazine
     named him the richest man in America in 1984 with a net worth of
     $2.2 billion. But in May, 1985, the Getty trust was split among
     other heirs, leaving poor Gordon with only $750 million. This
     makes David Packard of Silicon Valley's Hewlett-Packard the
     richest man in the Bay Area and the second richest in America with
     a fortune of $1.8 billion. His partner, William Hewlett, is number
     two in the Bay Area with $920 million. Getty is now in third place
     in the Bay Area and fourteenth nationally.

3   William C. Ralston. There was a shortage of minted gold coins and
     unfounded rumors were spreading that the banks were about to
     fail. To save his bank from panicky customers, Ralston exchanged
     his bank's gold bullion for minted gold coins. The exchange took
     place after midnight and without the federal government's
     knowledge.

4   Wilkes Bashford.

5   General William Sherman.

6   William Randolph Hearst.

7   Transamerica Pyramid.

8   Boz Scaggs.

9   Short for a colloquial term "nabob," meaning anyone of great
     wealth.

10   Eugene "Handsome Gene" Schmitz appealed his conviction,
     which was reversed by both the appelate and state supreme court.
     He returned to politics as a supervisor (1915–25), bidding
     unsuccessfully for mayor in 1915 and 1919.

LET US PRAY
Religion

1   Cecil Williams is pastor of this church.

2   This North Beach church was the first parish church in The City.

3   This is the largest Buddhist church in the United States.

4   Interdenominational Easter sunrise ceremonies are held at the foot of its famous cross.

5   On the corner of Lake and Arguello, this temple is the religious center for Reformed Judaism in San Francisco.

6   The first Russian cathedral in the United States was built on:
     a) Russian Hill.   b) Clement Street.
     c) Washington Square.
     d) Russia Street in the Mission District.

7   Name the Catholic church that has a Moslem mosque in its basement.

8   In April, 1985, this guru was sued by a former disciple for $5 million. The disciple claimed he had forced her into participating in sex orgies. Name the guru.

9   He runs St. Anthony's dining room.

10   In which church would you find the tower that has bells with names such as Sympathy, Isaiah, and Loving Kindness?

LET US PRAY
Religion

1   Glide Memorial.

2   St. Francis of Assisi. The parish was founded in 1849 and the present church was built in 1860. Its walls and towers survived the 1906 fire and are part of the present structure on Vallejo Street.

3   Buddha's Universal Church (Washington and Kearny). The church has a historical library for researching Chinese philosophy.

4   Mount Davidson.

5   Temple Emanu-El. The original site of the temple was on Sutter Street where the 450 Sutter Building stands today.

6   Holy Trinity Russian Orthodox Cathedral was built in 1868 on Powell Street, present site of the Washington Square Bar & Grill. Destroyed in the 1906 fire, the cathedral is now located at Green and Van Ness.

7   St. Ignatius. The church is on the University of San Francisco campus. The mosque was installed to accommodate foreign students.

8   Guru Da Free John, leader of a religious sect, Johannine Daist Communion, headquartered in San Rafael.

9   Reverend Floyd Lotito. The Franciscan has served at St. Anthony's for seventeen years.

10   Grace Cathedral. The cathedral is on the Nob Hill location of what once was Charles Crocker's estate.

AND IF ELECTED
Politicians

1   What was the nickname of Mayor James R. Rolph?

2   In September, 1984, this supervisor called for an investigation of The City's fluoridated water, saying it may be linked to AIDS and cancer.

3   In what years were city supervisors elected by district?

4   In October, 1976, President Gerald Ford and Jimmy Carter engaged in a televised debate in San Francisco. Where was it held?

5   In 1976, this controversial religious leader was appointed chairman of the San Francisco Housing Authority.

6   Who were the Paint Eaters?

7   In 1975, this man was defeated by George Moscone for mayor by only 4,443 votes.

8   In 1980, only two California counties voted for Jimmy Carter. One was San Francisco. Name the other.

9   In 1981, Jello Biafra, lead singer of the Dead Kennedys, was one of ten candidates on the ballot for mayor. In what place did he finish?
    a) second.   b) fourth.   c) seventh.   d) tenth.

10 He was the first native San Franciscan to be elected mayor.

AND IF ELECTED
Politicians

1   Sunny Jim.

2   Wendy Nelder.

3   1977 and 1979.

4   The Palace of Fine Arts Theatre.

5   Peoples Temple leader Jim Jones.

6   Supervisors during the term of Mayor Eugene Schmitz (1901–06) were so corrupt that it was said they would "eat the paint off a house!"

7   John Barbagelata lost by two percentage points.

8   Yolo County.

9   He finished fourth with 6,605 votes. Dianne Feinstein won the election.

10 Levi Richard Ellert (1893–95).

ANY WORD FROM THE GOVERNOR?
Prisoners

1   Corte Madera State Prison is the former name of what institution?

2   What Northern California prison now holds Charles Manson?

3   This was used as San Francisco's first jail.

4   Who was Dapper Duffy?

5   San Francisco's county prison is in San Bruno, which is in San Mateo County. Why?

6   Name the San Francisco sheriff who served a jail sentence while in office.

7   What's the maximum number of prisoners that San Quentin can accommodate by law?

8   When was the last execution at San Quentin?

9   This man was executed in San Quentin on May 2, 1960, after eight stays of execution and pleas for clemency from Albert Schweitzer, Marlon Brando and Brigitte Bardot.

10 In 1981, the first women's brig in U.S. naval history opened where?

ANY WORD FROM THE GOVERNOR?
Prisoners

1   San Quentin. The name was changed in 1879.

2   Vacaville.

3   The abandoned brig *Euphemia* in 1849. A jail was not built on dry land until 1851.

4   Clinton "Dapper" Duffy, San Quentin's warden from 1940 to 1951, was known for his extensive prison reforms and natty appearance.

5   Until 1856, San Francisco County stretched to Palo Alto. When the southern portion became San Mateo County, San Francisco retained ownership of three hundred acres near San Bruno. This city land was used for additional jail facilities in 1935.

6   In 1977 Sheriff Richard Hongisto served a five-day jail sentence for a contempt of court conviction stemming from his refusal to evict tenants of the International Hotel.

7   Thirty-three hundred.

8   Convicted murderer Aron Mitchell was executed in 1967.

9   Caryl Chessman.

10 Treasure Island.

SEX AND DRUGS AND ROCK AND ROLL

1   Carol Doda ushered in the topless era at this North Beach club.

2   Name the Berkeley actress/comedienne who made it big in 1984 with her one-woman Broadway show.

3   Who sang the national anthem at the 1984 All-Star Game in Candlestick Park?

4   What year did the Grateful Dead play a gig at the Hilton?

5   Name the porno queen whose first arrest took place at the Mitchell Brothers Theatre on February 1, 1984.

6   This rock impresario began his San Francisco career by writing press releases for the San Francisco Mime Troupe.

7   In the 1960s, Augustus Owsley Stanley III was famous for making the best. What did he make?

8   Because of the AIDS epidemic, he ordered The City's gay bath houses to be closed down.

9   Which rock video features an appearance by Willie Brown?

10   He was accused of killing a young actress, Virginia Rappe, in September, 1921, at the St. Francis Hotel during a wild orgy.

SEX AND DRUGS AND ROCK AND ROLL

1   The Condor Club. Davey Rosenberg, an employee at the club, put a Rudi Gernreich topless bathing suit on Carol, and the rest is history.

2   Whoopi Goldberg.

3   Huey Lewis and The News.

4   In 1969, as part of the Black and White Ball.

5   Marilyn Chambers. She was charged with lewd conduct and prostitution.

6   Bill Graham.

7   LSD. Acid connoisseurs were particularly fond of his Blue Barrels, Orange Sunshine and White Lightning varieties.

8   Dr. Mervyn Silverman, former San Francisco director of health.

9   "Layin' It On The Line" by the Jefferson Starship.

10   Roscoe "Fatty" Arbuckle. His first two trials ended in hung juries. His innocence was not declared until the third trial.

HIGH TRIVIA
Personalities

1   Name San Francisco's Silver Kings, also known as the Little Four.

2   Besides an American president, what head of state died at the Palace Hotel?

3   This famous American playwright had Gump's build a special bed for his dalmatian, Blemie.

4   Before she sang with Jefferson Airplane, Grace Slick performed with this early San Francisco rock group.

5   Name the Stanford band member who was run over by Cal running back Kevin Moen on the last play of the 1982 Big Game.

6   Name the two members of the Board of Supervisors who owned restaurants at Pier 39.

7   What good-luck charm did Enrico Caruso carry with him from the time the 1906 earthquake struck until he left San Francisco?

8   Where was Patty Hearst captured?

9   Name the Piedmont, California, family that, in addition to raising their own six children, has adopted fourteen handicapped children.

10   What is the name of Cyril Magnin's dog?

HIGH TRIVIA
Personalities

1   James G. Fair, John W. Mackay, William S. O'Brien and James J. Flood.

2   King David Kalakaua of Hawaii died there in 1891.

3   Eugene O'Neill.

4   The Great Society.

5   Trombonist Gary Tyrrell. He and the rest of the Stanford band ran onto the field prematurely, thinking the game was over.

6   Dan White (The Hot Potato) and Terry Francois (Francois's Creole Foods).

7   An autographed picture of President Theodore Roosevelt. In his fright, Caruso believed it would grant him special protection and privilege.

8   625 Morse Street, in San Francisco's Crocker-Amazon District.

9   The DeBolt family.

10   Tippy Canoe.

HISTORY

WAY BACK WHEN

1   Who founded San Francisco?

2   Although now thought to be a fraud, a "plate of brasse" was used as evidence to prove this explorer had set anchor on the Northern California coast. Name the explorer.

3   What was the name the Spanish settlers gave San Francisco?

4   He arrived in San Francisco in 1849 and declared himself the "Emperor of the United States and Protector of Mexico."

5   What is the oldest extant building in The City?

6   What section of The City is the site of San Francisco's first settlement?

7   San Francisco's first recorded earthquake occurred in this year.
        a) 1808.   b) 1849.   c) 1879.

8   Who built the first private residence in San Francisco?

9   Dupont was the name of San Francisco's oldest street. By what name do we know it today?

10   In the 1840s, this black Virgin Islander held the offices of city treasurer, school board chairman and captain of the port.

WAY BACK WHEN

1   Captain Juan Bautista de Anza founded San Francisco on March 29, 1776, near the present site of Fort Point, although it was another six months before he returned with his soldiers to settle here.

2   Sir Francis Drake. The brass plate was found in 1936, after an alleged 350-year absence, at Drake's Bay in Marin County. For years experts believed the plate to be authentic. Scientific testing in 1970, however, has cast serious doubt on its antiquity. Researchers believe the plate may contain an alloy found only in the American Midwest.

3   Yerba Buena, meaning good herb. The early settlers found a mintlike herb growing in profusion in The City.

4   Joshua Norton. Emperor Norton suffered from delusions after losing his fortune trying to corner the rice market.

5   Mission Dolores, completed in 1791.

6   The Presidio was settled on September 17, 1776. Mission Dolores was established twenty-one days later.

7   June 21, 1808.

8   Captain W. A. Richardson. The harbormaster built the first residence in Yerba Buena (San Francisco proper), in 1837, after living in a tent for two years.

9   Grant Avenue. The Chinese called Dupont Street *Du Pon Gai.*

10 William A. Leidesdorff. He was also a merchant, landowner and U.S. vice consul to Mexican Yerba Buena in 1845.

EUREKA!
The Gold Rush Years

1   What did it mean if a gold nugget would flatten when hit with a hammer?

2   In 1849, what was the monetary value of one ounce of gold?
    a) $4.   b) $16.   c) $32.   d)$102.

3   How did Henry D. Cogswell, D.D.S., become one of San Francisco's wealthiest men during the Gold Rush?

4   Once it was separated from all surrounding material, gold existed in these three forms.

5   The forty-niners used this slang expression to describe the hardship, disappointment and, most of all, the excitement of the gold fields.

6   Since 1849, how many of California's fifty-eight counties have had gold discoveries?
    a) 15.   b) 35.   c) 52.   d) all 58.

7   In 1849, this man left a successful confectionary business in Peru to prospect for gold in California.

8   As a boy, what infamous future actor performed Shakespearean plays in the gold fields with his father?

9   Gold miners of what nationality were known as Keskydees?

10 What Mother Lode town tried to secede from the Union during the Gold Rush in protest of mining taxes?

EUREKA!
The Gold Rush Years

1   During the Gold Rush, miners would test their findings by hitting the nuggets with a hammer. If the nugget shattered, it was fool's gold, if the nugget flattened out, it was genuine.

2   Sixteen dollars. The all-time high was $850 on January 19, 1980.

3   Cogswell made his fortune by accommodating the gold miners' desire for gold-capped front teeth, which were considered symbols of success.

4   Nuggets, dust and flakes.

5   Seeing the elephant.

6   Fifty-two. San Francisco was not one of them.

7   Domingo Ghirardelli, founder of the Ghirardelli Chocolate Company. His shop in Peru was next door to a cabinet shop owned by an American, James Lick.

8   John Wilkes Booth.

9   The French, because of the French question *qu'est-ce qu'il dit?* (What is he saying?).

10   Rough and Ready, near Grass Valley.

THE GOLD RUSH YEARS II

1   Where is the annual Frog Jumping Contest held?

2   What was the approximate value of the gold taken from the Mother
     Lode between 1849 and 1900?
          a) $5.6 million.   b) $23.7 million.   c) $50.4 million.
          d) $1.3 billion.

3   Lola Montez taught her to sing and dance. This protégée became a
     hit at age eight performing for miners in the Gold Country.

4   This Gold Rush town was first named Dry Diggins and later called
     Hangtown as a result of so many vigilante hangings. By what name
     is it known today?

5   He was the man who first discovered gold on John Sutter's mill.

6   Name the inventor of the waterwheel that used turbine principles
     to provide power. This is probably the most important invention to
     come out of the Gold Rush.

7   The Big Bonanza mine, said to be the largest pocket mine found in
     the Mother Lode, is in this town.

8   Name the author who wrote tales of the Gold Rush country, one of
     which is "Luck of Roaring Camp."

9   This famous figure of the Gold Rush left California in 1852 broken
     in spirit and bankrupt.

10   The largest nugget found during the Gold Rush period weighed:
          a) 59 pounds.   b) 36 pounds.   c) 195 pounds.
          d) 103 pounds.

THE GOLD RUSH YEARS II

1   Angels Camp during the Calaveras County Fair. It has been an official event since 1928.

2    $1.3 billion.

3   Lotta Crabtree. She traveled the Gold Country and was so popular the miners would literally shower her in gold. When she died her estate was valued at $4 million.

4   Placerville.

5   James Marshall, who was working on the tailrace of the lumber mill. He died a pauper.

6   Lester Pelton.

7   Sonora.

8   Bret Harte. For a time during the Gold Rush era, Harte lived in Tuttle Town and worked at a local store as a clerk.

9   John Sutter. Sutter was disappointed when his mill workers left his employ to join the Gold Rush. His own attempts at gold prospecting were ill-fated.

10   The largest nugget weighed 195 pounds.

COWBOYS AND INDIANS

1   On July 1, 1846, Captain John Fremont scaled the walls on the site of Fort Point to claim the Presidio for the United States. Name the adventurer who helped accomplish this feat.

2   The Pony Express, the famed mail delivery service, ended its first run in this Western city.

3   Called the Robin Hood of the Mexicans, this bandit robbed miners in the Gold Country. He was killed by Harry Love in 1853.

4   He was the most famous of all stagecoach robbers. While working he wore a flour sack over his head.

5   He lead the Mariposa Battalion, the first white explorers in Yosemite Valley.

6   At the height of its power in 1856, this group had nine thousand infantry, artillery and cavalry.

7   Who were the Costanoan, Coast Miwok and Wintun?

8   Based on a treaty with the U.S. government in 1868, Sioux warriors claimed this island as their own in March of 1964.

9   A statue of Catherine Tekakwitha, "Lily of the Mohawks," is located at Mission Dolores Cemetery. What does it commemorate?

10   Name San Francisco's first county sheriff.

COWBOYS AND INDIANS

1   Kit Carson. He accompanied Fremont on many of his expeditions and adventures.

2   Sacramento. The event was celebrated in San Francisco, when the horse and rider arrived here after a short trip on a riverboat down the Sacramento River.

3   Joaquin Murrieta. The bounty hunter Love, who killed Murrieta in 1853, was known for letting his prisoners escape so he could shoot them in the back.

4   Charles Boles alias Charles Bolton alias Black Bart. He was captured when a handkerchief he dropped at the scene of a crime was traced by its laundry mark.

5   James Savage.

6   Committee of Vigilance (Vigilantes). The committee was formed to protect the citizens from the lawlessness that prevailed in San Francisco.

7   Bay Area Indians.

8   Alcatraz Island.

9   This statue honors the more than five thousand Indians, victims of a smallpox epidemic, who are buried on mission grounds throughout California. Tekakwitha, a seventeenth-century Mohawk being considered for sainthood by the Catholic Church, lost her mother and brother to smallpox.

10   Colonel John C. Hays, former Texas Ranger. According to local history, he won the confidence of the voters because he looked so impressive on a horse. Hays became sheriff in 1850.

FLASH FROM THE PAST

1   Born John Bernardone in Italy's Perugia Province, his father changed his name to Francisco.

2   Eureka is not only a Northern California town, it is also the state slogan. What does the Greek word "eureka" mean?

3   Every state has two statues inside the nation's Capitol. One of California's is Father Junipero Serra. The other is a famous San Franciscan. Name him.

4   When Emperor Norton died in 1880, who paid for the funeral?

5   This man escaped from chains under water at Aquatic Park on August 26, 1907.

6   This building served as the temporary Hall of Justice and City Hall after the 1906 earthquake.

7   Our city flag, adopted on April 14, 1900, features this mythical bird.

8   During its construction, this famous building was called Halleck's Folly.

9   What famous architect designed the Palace of Fine Arts?
      a) Bernard Maybeck.   b) Timothy Pflueger.
      c) Robert Barrett.

10 Who is commemorated by a ninety-seven-foot-high monument in the center of Union Square?

FLASH FROM THE PAST

1   St. Francis, patron saint of San Francisco.

2   I have found it.

3   Thomas Starr King, first pastor of the First Unitarian Church, whose persuasive pro-Union oratory helped keep California in the Union during the Civil War. He is buried at the corner of Franklin and O'Farrell.

4   The Pacific Club, later known as the Pacific Union Club.

5   Harry Houdini escaped, in fifty-seven seconds.

6   Temple Sherith Israel, near California and Webster.

7   Phoenix. The phoenix was a symbol for San Francisco before the 1906 earthquake took place. The City had "risen out of the ashes" after six major fires between 1849 and 1851.

8   Montgomery Block, built by Henry W. Halleck in 1853. Skeptics didn't think San Francisco was ready for its first four-story building.

9   Bernard Maybeck for the Panama Pacific Exposition. It was originally built as a temporary structure and rebuilt in concrete in 1962.

10 Commodore George Dewey.

SHAKE, RATTLE AND ROLL
The 1906 Earthquake

1   According to U.C. seismologists who recorded the event, how intense was the quake?

2   Every year earthquake survivor Les Bulloch puts a coat of gold paint on the fire hydrant at 20th and Church streets. Why?

3   How many miles long is the San Andreas Fault?

4   What was the death toll after the quake?
       a) 239.   b) 674.   c) 1,016.   d) No one knows for sure.

5   Name the three fault lines in the San Francisco Bay Area.

6   This Northern California town is usually named as the epicenter of the 1906 earthquake.

7   Name the general who commanded the troops that policed San Francisco after the 1906 earthquake.

8   Under martial law, this famous actor was made to stack bricks in Union Square after the 1906 earthquake.

9   On what month and day did the 1906 earthquake occur?

10   Each year, on the anniversary of the 1906 earthquake, the survivors gather at which San Francisco landmark?

SHAKE, RATTLE AND ROLL
The 1906 Earthquake

1   The scientific instruments of the time rated the quake at IX, on a scale of I to X. The Richter scale measurement is 8.3.

2   This hydrant is believed to be the only one that functioned after the 1906 quake and is credited with saving the homes between 20th and 22nd streets from the ensuing fire.

3   Six hundred miles long and twenty miles deep.

4   No one knows for sure. Until recently the history books stated that the total was 674 (315 were killed outright, 6 were shot for crime, 1 was shot accidentally and 352 were missing and presumed dead). Evidence is coming to light that there may have been a cover-up as to the actual number killed in the quake. City officials reported the dead on the low side so as not to discourage tourism.

5   San Andreas, Hayward and Calaveras.

6   Olema.

7   Major General Frederick Funston.

8   John Barrymore.

9   April 18. The first tremor struck at 5:12 am.

10   Lotta's Fountain.

VICTORIA'S LEGACY
The Painted Ladies

1   Name the three principal styles of Victorian houses.

2   From 1850 to 1915 how many Victorians were built in San
     Francisco?
        a) 24,000.   b) 65,000.   c) 48,000.

3   This type of wood is predominant in Victorian houses in the West.

4   Why was the development of the wire nail so important to the
     Victorian style?

5   What is Lincrusta-Walton?

6   Many Victorian houses had two parlors. Social doctrine of the time
     prescribed that they be used in what way?

7   True or false: The bay window was created for San Francisco
     Victorians.

8   This Victorian on Franklin Street is the headquarters of The
     Foundation for San Francisco's Architectural Heritage.

9   Originally there were eight of these unusually shaped houses in
     San Francisco. Today only two remain.

10   Morton Street was once the red-light district of San Francisco. By
     what name do we know this street today?

VICTORIA'S LEGACY
The Painted Ladies

1   Italianate, San Francisco Stick and Queen Anne.

2   48,000.

3   Redwood. It was used for several reasons: The wood was plentiful, it can be easily molded into various shapes, it's soft and easy to cut yet strong enough to resist splintering when nailed.

4   Wire nails were easy to mass produce. It has been estimated that 65,000 nails were needed to build one five-room Stick house.

5   A linoleum-type wall covering, developed by Frederick Walton in England in 1877, that became the rage of Victorian decorators. It could be made to look like cast plaster, carved wood or even embossed leather.

6   The front parlor was used to receive any visitor. The rear parlor was reserved for intimate friends.

7   False. Bay windows are actually an ancient design and they did not become popular in San Francisco until the 1870s.

8   The Haas-Lilienthal House.

9   Octagon houses. One is at 1067 Green Street and the other at 2645 Gough Street.

10   Maiden Lane, off Union Square.

SAN FRANCISCO'S FIERY HERITAGE

1   Which of these was *not* one of San Francisco's first five volunteer fire departments:
a) Broderick One.   b) Embarcadero Two.   c) Howard Three.
d) California Four.   e) Knickerbocker Five.

2   What special privilege does San Francisco offer its fire chief?

3   How many times has the Cliff House burned down?

4   Firepersons' helmets are made from this material.

5   In what year did the firefighters strike occur?

6   What was the "ham and eggs" fire?

7   The Sutro Baths opened in 1896. What year did they burn down?

8   San Francisco has how many firehouses?

9   Why was San Francisco's first fire engine called the Martin Van Buren?

10   The cable car system was shut down after the 1906 earthquake, but the cars were put to good use. How?

SAN FRANCISCO'S FIERY HERITAGE

1   Embarcadero Two. The City's second volunteer fire department was named Protection Two.

2   Since 1922, The City's fire chiefs have been provided an official residence, located on Bush near Taylor. This is an honor not given any other city official.

3   Twice. Originally built in 1863, the Cliff House was destroyed by fire on Christmas Day, 1894. It was rebuilt by Adolph Sutro as a six-story gingerbread palace and survived the 1906 fire only to burn down in 1907. The present structure was built in 1908.

4   Leather. The helmets are so durable they are often passed down from father to son. For a short time, regulations required the firefighters to wear plastic helmets. A government law that melted away rather quickly.

5   August 20–21, 1975.

6   After the 1906 earthquake, downtown San Francisco was ablaze. But a larger fire was started by a woman cooking breakfast on Hayes Street near Gough. Her chimney flue was damaged and the flames spread from her home to the neighbors' houses. That morning she burned more than her toast. The Fire Department was of little help since they were occupied with the fire downtown.

7   Most illustrations portray Sutro Baths at the turn of the century, but they actually lasted until 1966. By that time, the pools had become an ice-skating rink.

8   Forty-one.

9   It derived its name because it was once used to water the lawn of President Martin Van Buren.

10   Homeless survivors of the 1906 fires put shingled walls on the cars and used them for temporary housing.

YOU CAN'T GET THERE FROM HERE
Landmarks Past

1   It was a thousand feet long, contained enough salt water to float the *Queen Mary*, and lifeguards patrolled it in rowboats.

2   Embarcadero Two overlooks the former site of the second Committee of Vigilance's headquarters. What was this building called?

3   Robin Williams began his career at this comedy night club, which closed in 1984.

4   Champions with names like Seabiscuit and Citation thrilled thousands here, until this track was replaced by a shopping center in the 1960s.

5   This famous department store was closed to make way for Neiman-Marcus.

6   The merry-go-round in this ten-acre amusement park, just south of the Cliff House, ran from 1916 to 1972. Name the park.

7   Burned to the ground in its seventieth year, it once had seven indoor pools, several restaurants, trapezes, water slides and a museum.

8   When this amusement center opened in the Mission District in 1866, it featured wild animals, both live and stuffed, an art gallery and a Chinese giant, over eight feet tall.

9   A Great Highway landmark from 1909 to 1972, Roald Amundsen sailed this ship through the Northwest Passage in 1903.

10   A marble archway is all that remains of the A. N. Towne mansion after fire razed Nob Hill on April 18, 1906. Where is the archway now?

YOU CAN'T GET THERE FROM HERE
Landmarks Past

1   Fleischacker Pool. When it opened in 1925, it was the largest swimming pool in the world, with 116,000 square feet of swimming area and 6.3 million gallons of water. It was filled with earth in 1984, after years of disuse.

2   Officially called Fort Vigilance, it was more commonly known as Fort Gunnybags, because of the sandbags that lined its outer walls.

3   Holy City Zoo.

4   Tanforan Race Track.

5   City of Paris (1896–1982).

6   Playland-at-the-Beach.

7   Sutro Baths. Built by Adolph Sutro in 1896, the seven pools ranged in temperature from extremely cold to 80 degrees.

8   Woodward's Gardens.

9   The *Gjoa*. This forty-seven-ton sloop was on display near the western boundary of Golden Gate Park until 1972, when it was returned to Amundsen's native Norway.

10 In Golden Gate Park, near Lloyd Lake on Kennedy Drive. This section of the park is called Portals of the Past.

TEN HUT!
The Military

1   During his military career, this future American president was a prisoner in the Benicia army stockade.

2   What was Fort Point used for during World War II?

3   In 1983, this 75,000-ton, 1122-foot warship ran aground on a sand bar in San Francisco Bay.

4   In World War I, this regiment was called "San Francisco's Own."

5   The last remnants of the original eighteenth-century Presidio pueblo are part of what present structure?

6   Three U.S. Navy warships have carried the name *San Francisco*. Name their types.

7   Who first built the aerial that provides uninterrupted radio reception through the Broadway Tunnel?

8   North Windmill in Golden Gate Park was rebuilt by volunteers from this military organization.

9   Who discovered San Francisco Bay: soldiers or sailors?

10   A headstone in Presidio National Cemetery bears the simple inscription: "Two Bits." Who was he?

TEN HUT!
The Military

1   Ulysses S. Grant. He was held overnight for being drunk and disorderly.

2   To house soldiers tending a submarine net stretched across the entrance to the bay.

3   The nuclear aircraft carrier *U.S.S. Enterprise.*

4   The 363rd Infantry, formed in 1917 as part of the 91st Division. The majority of this unit's enlisted men came from San Francisco.

5   A small portion of the Presidio's original adobe (circa 1790) is contained in the wall of the Presidio Officers Club. This adobe has been named as the oldest building in The City, but most scholars today believe it was built later than Mission Dolores (1782–91).

6   A cruiser, built in San Francisco in 1890; a heavy cruiser, launched at Mare Island in 1933; and the nuclear-powered attack submarine SSN-711, launched in 1980.

7   Engineers from the *U.S.S. Coral Sea.* Crew members from the *U.S.S. Carl Vinson* now maintain it.

8   The Seabees.

9   Soldiers, in 1769. After being overlooked by three famous sea explorers, a hunting party led by Sergeant Jose Ortega disembarked from Gaspar de Portola's ship and spotted San Francisco Bay from a hilltop. However, Portola's orders were to locate Monterey Bay, not find a new one, and the expedition promptly left.

10   An Indian scout who served with the U.S. Army.

EXPLOSIVE MOMENTS

1 When these two militant unionists were convicted of murder for
   the Preparedness Day bombing in 1916, the press called it the
   American Dreyfus Affair.

2 How many men did the two committees of Vigilance hang between
   1851 and 1856?
       a) 8.   b) 15.   c) 25.   d) At least 41, but perhaps more.

3 In 1859, a duel was fought between U.S. Senator David Broderick
   and Judge David S. Terry near Lake Merced. Who won?

4 In 1897, this famous inventor devised a plan to defend San
   Francisco Bay with a system of floating explosive devices that could
   be detonated using electricity.

5 In the 1870s, this sand-lot orator drew big crowds with his
   inflammatory remarks about the Chinese and the railroad
   magnates.

6 When this ship sank, on February 22, 1901, in San Francisco Bay,
   131 of her passengers died.

7 In order to connect the Sunset District with downtown San
   Francisco, two street-car tunnels were blasted through the hills.
   Name the tunnels.

8 In 1944, two ships full of munitions exploded in a small Bay Area
   port resulting in one of the greatest disasters in American history.
   Name the port.

9 This movie (not made in San Francisco) has the line, "If we make it,
   I'll buy a steak dinner at Ernie's."

10 On September 23, 1975, Sara Jane Moore fired a pistol at
   President Gerald Ford as he emerged from the St. Francis Hotel.
   Name the hero who grabbed her arm and diverted her aim.

EXPLOSIVE MOMENTS

1   Tom Mooney and Warren Billings. They were later believed to be innocent. Mooney was pardoned and Billings was released from prison, both in 1939.

2   Despite their ruthless reputations, the two committees of Vigilance only hung eight men in their five-year history.

3   Judge David S. Terry. Senator Broderick was shot to death.

4   Thomas Edison. The plan was never put into effect.

5   Denis Kearney.

6   *The City of Rio de Janeiro.* To this day the wreckage of the *Rio* has yet to be found.

7   Twin Peaks Tunnel, completed July 14, 1917, and the Duboce Street Tunnel, completed October 21, 1928.

8   Port Chicago. The shock waves were so intense many people assumed it was an earthquake. The bodies of the 321 victims were never found.

9   *The High and the Mighty.* The screenplay was written by Ernest Gann, who was quite fond of the restaurant.

10   Oliver Sipple.

SCHOOL DAZE
Local Education

1   Name San Francisco's only Bible college.

2   This local school is nationally famous for its "65 Club."

3   This is the oldest art school in the West.

4   In 1985, this ninety-eight-year-old San Francisco college relocated to Silicon Valley.

5   Name the first night law school in the state of California.

6   In this college's earlier years, it was compulsory for each student to walk one mile in the fresh air, daily.

7   St. Ignatius Academy is now known by what name?

8   What did Stanford call its sports teams before they changed their name to the Cardinal?

9   Name the Contra Costa County college that originally began on a hilltop just south of the Mission District.

10 What percentage of America's Nobel laureates live in the Bay Area?
       a) 5 percent.   b) 10 percent.   c) 20 percent.   d) 25 percent.

SCHOOL DAZE
Local Education

1 Simpson College, 801 Silver Avenue. Founded in Seattle in 1921, the school moved to San Francisco in 1955.

2 Hastings School of Law. Its 65 Club is composed of distinguished law professors and jurists recruited to its faculty after reaching the age of mandatory retirement at other institutions.

3 The San Francisco Art Institute. This school was founded in 1871 by the San Francisco Art Association and for many years was known as the California School of Fine Arts. Before it acquired its present Russian Hill site, the school's previous locations included a loft above a butcher shop on Pine Street and the Mark Hopkins mansion on Nob Hill.

4 Cogswell College.

5 Golden Gate School of Law.

6 Mills College.

7 The University of San Francisco. It began in a one-room wooden structure on the present site of the Emporium on Market Street in 1855.

8 The Indians.

9 St. Mary's College, established 1862. Unable to expand on its original location, it moved to Oakland in 1889, and then to Moraga in 1928.

10 Twenty percent, according to a 1979 University of California survey. In 1985, the Bay Area had twenty-one Nobel recipients.

HAPPY DAZE ARE HERE AGAIN
Political Conventions in San Francisco

1   How many major national political conventions have been held in San Francisco?

2   He was nominated for president at the Republican convention in 1964.

3   Who was the keynote speaker at the Democratic convention in 1984?

4   At the 1920 Democratic convention, there was talk of nominating a woman for vice president, Mrs. Peter Olsen of Minnesota. Who was the vice-presidential nominee that year?

5   Reporters from Walt Disney covered this San Francisco convention for the Mickey Mouse Club.

6   Name the city that was the main contender with San Francisco for the 1984 Democratic convention.

7   Where in San Francisco was the 1920 Democratic convention held?

8   Who was the head of The City's host committee for the 1984 Democratic convention?

9   Name the keynote speaker for the 1956 Republican convention.

10   What was the official wine of the 1984 Democratic convention?

HAPPY DAZE ARE HERE AGAIN
Political Conventions in San Francisco

1   Four. The Democratic convention in 1920, the 1956 and 1964 Republican conventions and the 1984 Democratic convention.

2   Barry Goldwater. At this convention he uttered what was probably his most famous quote: "Extremism in the defense of liberty is no vice . . . moderation in the defense of justice is no virtue."

3   Mario Cuomo, governor of New York.

4   A newcomer, Franklin Delano Roosevelt.

5   The 1956 Republican convention. The Mouseketeers liked Ike.

6   Chicago.

7   The Civic Auditorium.

8   Nancy Pelosi, former chair of the state Democratic party.

9   Governor Arthur B. Langlie of Washington.

10 A Napa Valley 1982 Cabernet Sauvignon from Vineyard Wine Cellars.

THE ROCK
Alcatraz

1   Name the Birdman of Alcatraz.

2   J. Edgar Hoover is said to have personally supervised the capture of this Alcatraz inmate.

3   This was the average amount of time served by inmates of Alcatraz.
     a) 3 years.   b) 9 years.   c) 18 years.   d) 25 years.

4   When Alcatraz became a federal prison in 1934, it had been designed for "maximum punishment with minimum privilege." Perhaps the harshest rule of all was this general prison policy from 1934 to 1937.

5   Despite the harsh discipline, Alcatraz had what two luxuries?

6   How many of The Rock's thirty-nine escapees are still unaccounted for?

7   These were Alcatraz's first civilian prisoners.

8   How far is The Rock from the mainland?

9   Alcatraz is a Spanish word meaning?

10   Frank C. Weatherman said: "Alcatraz was never no good to nobody." What is his distinction?

THE ROCK
Alcatraz

1 Robert Stroud spent seventeen years in solitary confinement on Alcatraz. In all, he spent fifty-four of his seventy-two years in prison.

2 Alvin "Creepy" Karpis, who had been involved in the kidnapping of the Hamms Brewery heir. It is said that when the Giants games were allowed to be broadcast on Alcatraz, Karpis was especially fond of the Hamms jingle.

3 Nine years.

4 No talking.

5 Hot showers and the best food in the federal prison system. Government regulations set a minimum of 2,100 calories daily, but Alcatraz inmates received from 3,100 to 3,600.

6 Three. Twenty-six were recaptured, seven were shot and killed, one was drowned and two are presumed drowned.

7 Fifteen Southern sympathizers who were imprisoned at the outbreak of the Civil War. Alcatraz's first inmates were soldiers transferred from the Presidio stockade.

8 1.5 miles.

9 Pelican.

10 He was the last inmate to leave Alcatraz.

FLASH FROM THE RECENT PAST

1   He was the only president of the United States to die in San Francisco.

2   In 1924, the first transcontinental air mail service was completed between New York and San Francisco. Where did the plane land?

3   In 1929, two years after becoming an aviation legend, his plane became stuck in the mud while attempting a takeoff from San Francisco's airport. Name the pilot.

4   Name the privately owned water company that preceded The City's municipal water system.

5   Name the Southern Pacific train that ran between San Francisco and Monterey until 1971.

6   In San Francisco, as in other cities, telephone exchanges once had names and not just numbers. Identify these prefixes:
     a) YU.   b) EX.   c) SU.   d) JO.   e) SK.   f) DO.

7   What was Bloody Thursday?

8   He was the only mayor of San Francisco to be born in Greece.

9   On August 16, 1942, U.S. Navy patrol blimp L-8 crashed at 432 Bellevue Avenue in Daly City. What was peculiar about the incident?

10   He was released from prison on January 6, 1984.

FLASH FROM THE RECENT PAST

1   Warren Harding died August 2, 1923, at the Palace Hotel. His funeral was held in City Hall's great rotunda.

2   Crissy Field at the Presidio.

3   Charles Lindbergh. The Lone Eagle, his thirty-two passengers and plane were rescued by a tractor.

4   Spring Valley Water Works, named after a small spring near Washington and Mason streets. In 1928, San Francisco voters approved its purchase.

5   The Del Monte Special.

6   Yukon, Exbrook, Sutter, Jordan, Skyline, Douglas.

7   July 5, 1934, when dockworkers and police battled in the streets during a waterfront strike. Two longshoremen were shot in the back and killed, and hundreds were injured.

8   George Christopher (Christopheles), mayor from 1956 to 1964.

9   The crew had vanished. The parachutes and rubber raft were still on board and the radio was operable. There was no evidence of malfunction, struggle aboard ship or attack from outside. The door had been latched open, but an investigation concluded that there was no reason for voluntary abandonment. Both crew men were experienced pilots and are still listed as missing.

10 Former Supervisor Dan White, convicted murderer of Mayor George Moscone and Supervisor Harvey Milk.

THEY TURNED ON, TUNED IN AND DROPPED OUT
Haight-Ashbury in the 1960s

1   A member of a famous British rock group toured the Haight in the 1960s with his wife Patty. Name him.

2   "May the Good Lord Shut Your Mouth and Open Your Mind" was the motto of this ballroom famous for rock concerts in the sixties.

3   This Haight-Ashbury group handed out free food in the Panhandle of Golden Gate Park.

4   He had acid tests with his Merry Pranksters.

5   This student radical at U.C. Berkeley helped organize the 1967 Human Be-In. He later became one of the "Chicago Seven."

6   In 1966, one kilo (2.2 pounds) of quality marijuana sold for:
        a) $150.   b) $80.   c) $500.   d) $350.

7   Bill Graham opened the Fillmore on December 10, 1965, and featured this rock group.

8   Name the Haight's own psychedelic newspaper.

9   Originally, this rock band was called the Warlocks.

10   Where was Hippie Hill?

THEY TURNED ON, TUNED IN AND DROPPED OUT
Haight-Ashbury in the 1960s

1   George Harrison of the Beatles.

2   Avalon Ballroom.

3   The Diggers. Founded in the Haight by Emmett Grogan and Peter Berg, the Diggers were responsible for feeding hundreds of hungry people each day. The Digger organization is nothing new; it dates back as far as seventeenth-century England.

4   Ken Kesey.

5   Jerry Rubin.

6   Eighty dollars.

7   Jefferson Airplane. Besides the Airplane, the Fillmore hosted rock concerts with groups such as the Grateful Dead and Big Brother and the Holding Company.

8   *The San Francisco Oracle.* The rainbow-colored paper was sprayed with jasmine perfume as each issue came off the press.

9   The Grateful Dead.

10   Golden Gate Park off Kezar Drive.

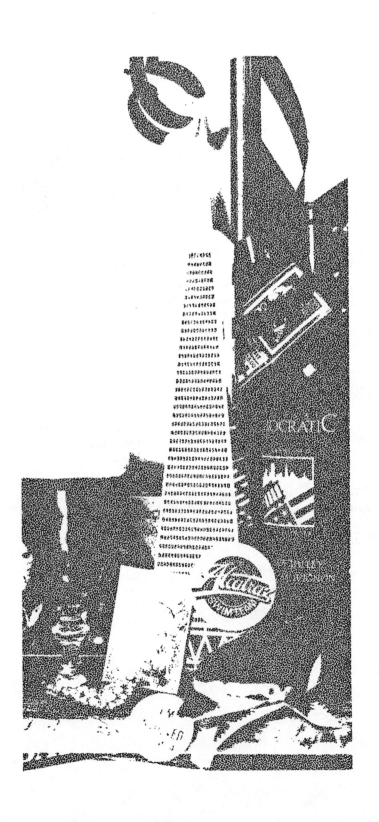

ONLY IN
SAN FRANCISCO

BAY AREA ORIGINALS

1   Where was the "Chinese" fortune cookie invented?

2   What is the name of the dessert created especially for Queen Elizabeth II during her visit to San Francisco?

3   This man is credited with inventing Pisco Punch, San Francisco's only native drink.

4   Name the East Bay lake that was the first wildlife sanctuary in the United States.

5   A truly San Franciscan creation, this treat was invented at Playland-at-the-Beach in 1928.

6   In 1983 and 1984, a novelty Christmas song performed by a Sonoma County couple pushed Bing Crosby's "White Christmas" from the top spot of the season's most requested songs. Name the song.

7   What is Lactobacillus sanfrancisco?

8   Where is Rice-A-Roni (The San Francisco Treat!) made?

9   What was Ghirardelli Square before it was a chocolate factory?

10   Who was the Gold Rush entrepreneur who cut his first pair of pants from a canvas tent?

BAY AREA ORIGINALS

1   The Japanese Tea Garden. The fortune cookie was invented by Makato Hagiwara, whose family operated the Tea Garden from 1895 to 1942. Local Chinese restaurants adopted it around the turn of the century.

2   Aurora Pacifica, created by the St. Francis Hotel.

3   Duncan "Pisco John" Nichol invented it at the Bank Exchange Bar, in the Montgomery Block Building. The recipe died with him.

4   Lake Merritt.

5   The Its-It, a scoop of ice cream sandwiched between two oatmeal cookies, dipped in chocolate, then frozen.

6   "Grandma Got Run Over by a Reindeer," performed by Elmo and Patsy. Since its introduction in 1979, it has sold over a million records. San Franciscan Randy Brooks wrote the lyrics.

7   The micro-organism that is the secret of The City's sourdough bread starter.

8   Rice-A-Roni has always been made in San Leandro. In 1961, an advertising campaign began using the slogan "The San Francisco Treat" in order to capitalize on The City's reputation for fine restaurants.

9   The Pioneer Woolen Mill. It manufactured uniforms and blankets for the Union Army during the Civil War.

10 Levi Strauss. Merchant Strauss realized that miners needed durable trousers and converted his tents into what we now know as Levis.

VITAL STATISTICS
Numbers, Numbers, Numbers

1   What are Carol Doda's measurements?

2   How long is the Bay to Breakers foot race?

3   A cable car moves at only one speed. How fast does it go?
    a) 5 mph.   b) 8 mph.   c) 9.5 mph.   d) 12 mph.

4   How far is the drop from the Golden Gate Bridge?
    a) 100 feet.   b) 220 feet.   c) 320 feet.   d) 500 feet.

5   San Francisco occupies how many square miles?
    a) 20.2.   b) 46.38.   c) 75.36.   d) 79.4.

6   What percentage of the San Francisco Bay has been filled in?
    a) 10 percent.   b) 15 percent.   c) 25 percent.
    d) 30 percent.

7   This was the final score of Super Bowl XIX.

8   What is the width of the Golden Gate?
    a) .5 miles.   b) 1 mile.   c) 1.5 miles.   d) 2 miles.

9   How many Irish coffees does the Buena Vista Cafe sell on an
    average day?
    a) 250.   b) 550.   c) 1000.   d) 2000.

10 What percentage of San Francisco's single men are gay?
    a) 10 percent.   b) 40 percent.   c) 50 percent.
    d) 100 percent.

VITAL STATISTICS
Numbers, Numbers, Numbers

1   Carol Doda measures 44-22-36.

2   7.46 miles. In 1979, the distance was decreased from 7.6 miles, to facilitate the incredible jam of runners at the finish line at the Great Highway.

3   9.5 miles per hour.

4   The drop is 222 feet at low tide, the equivalent of a nineteen-story building.

5   46.38 square miles.

6   Approximately 30 percent, according to the last survey taken by the U.S. Army Corps of Engineers. Over 70 percent of the bay is shallower than 18 feet, which makes it so easy to fill in.

7   San Francisco 38, Miami 16.

8   About one mile.

9   Two thousand on an average day, 363 days a year.

10   40 percent. According to a marketing research survey conducted in 1984, two out of five.

QUESTIONS FOR NATIVES ONLY

1   Name the mechanical fat lady at Playland.

2   What was the Hippie Hop?
          a) bus tour of the Haight-Ashbury, 1967.
          b) drug-induced dance.   c) panhandling technique.

3   How many Yet Wah Restaurants are there on Clement Street?

4   What large object hangs over the fireplace at the Merchants
       Exchange Club?

5   There are three types: siren, diaphragm and diaphone.

6   How many golf courses are there in San Francisco?

7   This movie theater was named by *Time* magazine as a Notable
       Design Achievement of 1984.

8   This comic strip was being syndicated in twenty-five newspapers
       when the cartoonist decided to write it only for the *San Francisco
       Chronicle*. Name the cartoon series and the artist.

9   Where are San Francisco's three operating merry-go-rounds?

10   What was the face value of a ticket for Super Bowl XIX?

QUESTIONS FOR NATIVES ONLY

1   Laughing Sal.

2   A Gray Line bus tour of Haight-Ashbury in 1967. It was touted as
       "a safari through Psychodelphia, and the only foreign tour within
       the continental limits of the United States." Price: Six dollars.

3   Two: 2140 Clement and 1829 Clement. There was once a third,
       the original location, which closed.

4   An alleged bone from a whale's penis.

5   Fog signals. The sirens have a single pitch contralto. The
       diaphragm or air horn blasts a single pitch baritone sound. The
       diaphone can create a variety of sounds and at maximum power can
       bellow out at two hundred decibels.

6   Eight: Presidio, Lincoln, Golden Gate Park, San Francisco Golf
       Club, McLaren Municipal, Harding, Olympic Country Club
       (Two).

7   Galaxy Theatre, designed by architects Kaplan/McLaughlin/Diaz.

8   *Travels with Farley*, created by Phil Frank. He wanted the strip to
       focus on local issues affecting the Bay Area.

9   Pier 39, Golden Gate Park and the San Francisco Zoo.

10   Sixty dollars.

THREE DOT JOURNALISM
Herb Caen

1   Who said of Caen: "This kid is the best imitation of me I ever saw."?

2   What was Herb's first job with the *San Francisco Chronicle*?

3   This weird contributor to Caen's columns is sometimes accused of being Herb himself.

4   Caen coined this word for the hip generation of the 1950s.

5   Where did Herb Caen's first columns appear?

6   He was Herb's assistant for thirty-six years; name him.

7   When this hotel was built in downtown San Francisco, Caen called it: "The box the Jack Tar came in." Name the hotel.

8   What is Caen's claim to being a native San Franciscan?

9   When Caen left the *Chronicle* to write for the *Examiner*, how many years was he with that paper?

10   Caen was once sued and lost an invasion of privacy case. What were the circumstances?

THREE DOT JOURNALISM
Herb Caen

1   New York columnist Walter Winchell.

2   At age twenty, Caen was hired to write the radio column as Dinty Doyle's replacement. Doyle left the job to write in New York.

3   Strange de Jim.

4   Beatnik. It has been said that Caen takes greater pride for dubbing the Golden Gate Bridge "The car strangled spanner."

5   In his Sacramento High School newspaper. Herb called the column "Corridor Gossip" and used the nom de plume Raisen Caen.

6   Jerry Bundsen. He stopped working with Herb when he grew weary of the commute from his San Carlos home.

7   The Hilton Hotel on O'Farrell. The Jack Tar Hotel was a favorite target of Caen's sarcasm. Located on Van Ness and Geary, it is now called the Cathedral Hill Hotel.

8   Although he was born in Sacramento, Caen has stated that he was conceived while his parents were visiting the 1915 Panama-Pacific Exposition in San Francisco.

9   Caen was with the *Examiner* a total of eight years (1950–58).

10   Herb printed in his column that a chiropractor practiced at night and drove a Yellow Cab during the day. The chiropractor/cabbie won the case on the grounds that item harmed his image as a professional. He won a $10,000 judgement.

THE STREETS OF SAN FRANCISCO

1   What two streets were named after a milkman and his wife?

2   These two San Francisco streets were named after streets in New York.

3   This street was once the dividing line between San Francisco and the Presidio.

4   Name San Francisco's longest street.

5   Lombard has been called the world's crookedest street. How many turns does it have?

6   Which San Francisco street is the widest?

7   Known as "Washerwoman's Lagoon," this street was named for a pond.

8   This surveyor named the streets in San Francisco.

9   Many of The City's street intersections have large circles outlined with bricks. Why?

10   San Francisco does not have a Thirteenth Avenue. Name the street that runs between Twelfth and Fourteenth avenues, through both the Sunset and Richmond districts.

THE STREETS OF SAN FRANCISCO

1   Gough and Octavia streets. Charles H. Gough was a city milkman in the 1850s, working the route on a horse with milk cans tied to the saddle. In 1885, he and his wife were members of a citizens committee that named the streets of the Western Addition, naming two streets after themselves. Contrary to popular myth, Octavia was not the name of his horse.

2   Greenwich and Broadway.

3   Divisadero Street. In the 1850s, the Presidio army reservation was much larger than it is today.

4   Mission (7.29 miles).

5   Eight.

6   Van Ness Avenue (125 feet).

7   Laguna Street.

8   Jasper O'Farrell. When O'Farrell plotted out Market Street, he wanted a new road that would parallel the old trail from Yerba Buena Cove to Mission Dolores. He didn't realize that by plotting Market on a 45-degree angle he would cause headaches for builders for years to come.

9   The brick circles outline underground cisterns. San Francisco has 151 of them, each containing an average of 75,000 gallons of water to be saved for fire emergencies. When repaving, the street department tries to maintain the circular outline, in case firemen ever need to punch a hole in the top.

10   Funston Avenue.

BAY AREA BUMMERS

1   This certificate costs thirty dollars at City Hall and it could last a lifetime.

2   You parked your Chevy in a red zone on Union Street. You must pay $53.25 to this company for towing your car.

3   You dropped your playbill on the sidewalk in front of the Curran and one of San Francisco's finest gives you a ticket for littering. How much will it cost you?

4   What is the police emergency phone number?

5   You are coming back from Stinson Beach on Sunday. How much is the toll on the Golden Gate Bridge?

6   By what percentage could your landlord legally raise your rent in each year?

7   You are walking Fido in Golden Gate Park. There is a city ordinance requiring you to use a pooper-scooper. True or false?

8   It's two o'clock in the morning and you are waiting for the #1 California bus. How long will you have to wait until the bus comes by?

9   You call the Fire Department and the firemen knock down your front door with their axes. Who must pay to replace the door?

10   The National Weather Service will tell you that the average annual rainfall in San Francisco is:
    a) 17.54 inches.   b) 20.66 inches.   c) 27.93 inches.

BAY AREA BUMMERS

1   A marriage license.

2   ABC Towing.

3   Fourteen dollars.

4   911. It is also the emergency number for the Fire Department, ambulance, paramedics and Coast Guard.

5   One dollar. The toll is one dollar Sunday through Thursday and two dollars Friday and Saturday.

6   The legal range is 4 percent minimum to 7 percent maximum. The range is tied to the cost of living index.

7   True.

8   A long time; the #1 California doesn't run after midnight.

9   You do. When you call the Fire Department, it is understood that you are giving the firefighters your implied consent to take actions to control the fire.

10   20.66 inches.

THE OLDEST, THE BIGGEST, THE FIRST

1   Name the oldest sourdough bakery in The City.

2   Where was the first McDonald's in San Francisco?

3   What is San Francisco's longest building?

4   Name The City's largest law firm.

5   Which is San Francisco's oldest men's club?

6   Every year, this Marin County town has the most rainfall in the Bay Area.

7   What is the highest man-made structure in The City?

8   Name the first paved road in San Francisco.

9   This San Francisco radio personality is reputed to have the world's largest T-shirt collection.

10   Who created the world's largest American flag made of balloons? It was displayed at City Hall during the opening of Fleet Week in 1984.

THE OLDEST, THE BIGGEST, THE FIRST

1   Boudin Bakery, established in 1849.

2   McDonald's opened in 1971 at 1201 Ocean in the Ingleside District.

3   China Basin Building, 850 feet.

4   Pillsbury, Madison and Sutro. In 1985, the firm employed 380 lawyers.

5   Pacific Union Club on Nob Hill.

6   Kentfield. According to a recent U.S. meteorological survey, in 1981 it had over twice the rainfall of San Francisco. In 1983, it had over four times as much.

7   Sutro Tower, the television tower on Twin Peaks.

8   Kearny between Clay and Washington, paved in 1854.

9   Carter B. Smith of KSFO.

10 Charlotte Mailliard, as recorded in *The Guinness Book of Records*.

HALFWAY TO THE STARS
The Cable Cars

1   The first cable car ran on what street?

2   This important event on October 1, 1964, helped assure the cable cars' perpetuation.

3   How many cable car turntables are running today?

4   Before the development of the cable car made Andrew Hallidie famous, what was his occupation?

5   In 1964, newlyweds Linda Bird Johnson Robb (President Johnson's daughter) and Charles Robb were ejected from a cable car for doing what?

6   All of the cable car track was replaced during the shutdown of 1982–83. Where was the new track manufactured?

7   What is the average yearly passenger load of the cable car system?

8   In April of 1963, this incident ended ninety-two years of sexual discrimination on the cable cars.

9   Who is Ding Dong Daddy?

10   What do cable car operators call the cable?

HALFWAY TO THE STARS
The Cable Cars

1   Andrew Hallidie made the first cable car run down Clay Street between Jones and Kearny, on August 2, 1873.

2   Congress declared them a National Historic Landmark.

3   Four: Powell-Market, Bay-Taylor, Beach-Hyde and the Washington-Mason car barn.

4   He manufactured wire rope for suspension bridges and tramways.

5   Eating ice cream cones.

6   America's rolling landmark now runs on track made in France. The French company was the lowest bidder.

7   The last estimate, made in 1982, was over thirteen million.

8   When a nineteen-year-old Berkeley coed defied the long-standing prohibition against women riding on the running boards, the gripman refused to start the car. Investigating police found no city law to support this tradition, and women have ridden on the steps ever since.

9   The title given the annual winner of the cable car bell-ringing competition.

10   The rope.

SANFRANCISCOLINGO
The Native Dialect

1   In The City, the ensemble of white shoes with a matching white belt is referred to as what?

2   Where is South of the Slot?

3   What is the Wall Street of the West?

4   Known for its clientele of attractive young people who seem to be there to pick up more than a loaf of bread, where is the "Social Safeway"?

5   Because of its frequent use as a brush-off in social conversation, the phrase, "Let's have lunch sometime," is called what?

6   What bus line is called "The Orient Express"?

7   When old-timers say "Meet me under the clock," they mean where?

8   Why is the 450 Sutter Building called "450 Suffer"?

9   What is Lottie's Pump?

10 What are the greensheet and the pink pages?

SANFRANCISCOLINGO
The Native Dialect

1   A full Cleveland. The wearing of just the white belt or white shoes alone is called a half Cleveland.

2   South of Market Street.

3   Montgomery Street.

4   The Marina Safeway, on Marina Boulevard and Buchanan.

5   The California kiss-off.

6   The #30 Stockton.

7   The lobby of the St. Francis Hotel.

8   Most of the building is occupied by doctors' and dentists' offices.

9   Lotta's Fountain, at Market and Kearny.

10   The *San Francisco Chronicle* sports section and the *Datebook* Sunday entertainment section.

DON'T JUMP
The Golden Gate Bridge

1   Who supervised the building of the Golden Gate Bridge?

2   The "Pathfinder" named the Golden Gate Strait. Name the Pathfinder.

3   In what year did the Golden Gate Bridge open?

4   What color paint is used on the Golden Gate Bridge?

5   The Golden Gate Bridge is designed to sway safely twenty-seven feet from side to side. How far has it ever swayed?

6   How many workers were killed during the bridge's construction?

7   Who said, "San Francisco needs that bridge. We will take the bonds."?

8   How long is the bridge?

9   Some people have jumped off the bridge and lived to tell the tale. How many?

10   In April, 1960, the bridge was closed to all traffic except to cars in this foreign dignitary's entourage. Name him.

DON'T JUMP
The Golden Gate Bridge

1   Joseph Strauss. Just below the toll plaza, on the San Francisco side, is a statue of Strauss.

2   John C. Fremont, adventurer and explorer. Fremont was instrumental in fulfilling President Polk's doctrine of Manifest Destiny: that the United States would extend from the Atlantic to the Pacific.

3   May 27, 1937. The first day it opened to pedestrian traffic only; on May 28 cars were allowed to cross the bridge.

4   International orange. It takes ten thousand gallons of the rust-preventive color to paint the bridge.

5   On December 1, 1951, gale winds reached seventy miles an hour. The bridge swayed twenty-four feet from side to side, and the roadway pitched five feet up and down. The bridge sustained only minor damage.

6   Eleven. The first worker died on October 21, 1936, when a derrick toppled and pinned him down. Ten workers died on February 17, 1937, when their wooden platform fell to the waters below.

7   A. P. Giannini of the Bank of America. While other bankers were skeptical, he provided Strauss with the financing necessary to build the bridge.

8   1.7 miles.

9   At least twelve. Bridge officials claim that most suicides drive to the bridge rather than walk.

10   President Charles de Gaulle, of France. Even though the traffic on the bridge was halted in his honor, his driver still had to pay the twenty-five-cent toll.

91

THE GOLDEN GATE'S BIGGER BROTHER
The Bay Bridge

1   Why is the Bay Bridge considered one of the seven engineering wonders of the world?

2   There are virtually no suicides from the Bay Bridge. Why?

3   The Bay Bridge converted from two-way traffic to one-way traffic on each deck in what year?

4   How many gallons of paint does it take to cover the Bay Bridge?
    a) 5,000.   b) 12,000.   c) 18,000.   d) 50,000.

5   Treasure Island was built for the Golden Gate International Exposition in 1939. After the exposition closed, engineers intended the island would be used for what purpose?

6   How many times has the Bay Bridge been hit by airplanes?

7   Name the natural island that anchors the San Francisco and Oakland sections of the Bay Bridge.

8   The Bay Bridge is the longest steel high-level bridge in the world. What is its length, including approaches?

9   Name the three types of spans used in the Bay Bridge.

10 Originally cars were permitted only on the upper level of the Bay Bridge. How was the lower level used?

THE GOLDEN GATE'S BIGGER BROTHER
The Bay Bridge

1   On the San Francisco side of the bridge, the monstrous island that roots it to the bay floor is larger than the Great Pyramid and has more concrete than the Empire State Building.

2   The Bay Bridge has no pedestrian walkways.

3   1963.

4   Eighteen thousand gallons.

5   Treasure Island was slated to become San Francisco International Airport. The City traded the island to the U.S. Navy for land south of Candlestick.

6   Twice. Both incidents, in 1968 and 1942, involved U.S. Navy aircraft.

7   Yerba Buena Island.

8   8.25 miles. Only about half of that is over water.

9   Suspension, cantilever and truss.

10   The lower level was used for trucks and electric commuter trains.

EGOS AND EYESORES
Landmarks

1   This government building at Sansome and Pine was built on the site of The City's first prison.

2   In 1929, she left funds to have a memorial built for volunteer firemen.

3   It has been estimated that on an average working day in 1914, this many commuters passed through the Ferry Building.
    a) 10,000.   b) 50,000.   c) 100,000.

4   This grand hotel stood at Market and Powell before it burned in 1898.

5   Built in 1891, this office building is San Francisco's oldest "skyscraper."

6   This is probably the only building in the Financial District where you will find bulls and bears. It's on the corner of Pine and Sansome.

7   What is the country's only mobile national landmark?

8   The Musee Mechanique is located in this historic San Francisco landmark.

9   One-third of our country's gold reserve was housed here in 1939.

10   San Francisco has had three cathedrals named St. Mary's. Old St. Mary's (1854) is at California and Grant. St. Mary's Cathedral (1970) is at 1111 Gough. Where was the other one?

EGOS AND EYESORES
Landmarks

1   The Federal Reserve Bank.

2   Lillie Hitchcock Coit. She endowed Coit Tower on Telegraph Hill.

3   Before the Golden Gate and Bay bridges were completed, as many as 100,000 people passed through the building each day.

4   The Baldwin Hotel. Lucky Baldwin, a millionaire of dubious reputation, built the hotel to rival the Palace. When his hotel burned in 1898, Baldwin had no insurance on the building.

5   The Mills Building at Bush and Montgomery. It is the only example of the Chicago School of architecture to survive the 1906 fire, although it was severely damaged.

6   Pacific Stock Exchange.

7   The cable cars were declared a national landmark by Congress on October 1, 1964.

8   The Cliff House.

9   The Old Mint at Fifth and Mission streets.

10   St. Mary's Cathedral (1891) at Van Ness and O'Farrell. It survived the 1906 fire, but burned down in 1962.

THE BIGGEST INDUSTRY
Tourism

1   This is the most popular tourist attraction in San Francisco.

2   How much does it cost to spend one night in the Fairmont's penthouse suite?

3   Name the Geary Street shop that carries close to three hundred out-of-town newspapers and magazines.

4   What question ranks number one, as the most often asked by tourists?

5   Which airline carried the most passengers into San Francisco International in 1984?

6   This San Francisco-based shipping firm has a fleet of three luxury cruise ships: *Sea*, *Star* and *Sky*.

7   Name the unique North Beach shop that's the place to visit if you want to drop the folks back home a line.

8   What are the two ferry services that can take you from San Francisco to Sausalito?

9   According to the San Francisco Convention and Visitors Bureau, most San Francisco visitors come from this American city.

10   This is reputed to be the most often photographed site in San Francisco.

THE BIGGEST INDUSTRY
Tourism

1   The cable cars.

2   Three thousand dollars plus tax. Besides the fully stocked bar, three bedrooms and a billiard room, the suite comes with sixteen-hour maid and butler service.

3   Harold's Hometown News.

4   "How do I get to Fisherman's Wharf?" According to an informal survey of the concierges in San Francisco's hotels.

5   United Airlines.

6   Royal Viking Lines.

7   The Postcard Palace on Columbus Avenue. The shop stocks thousands of postcards from the sublime to the ridiculous.

8   The Golden Gate Ferry and the Red and White Fleet.

9   Los Angeles.

10   The Golden Gate Bridge.

PARTY HEARTY
Bay Area Celebrations

1   Only the Japanese Tea Garden and the Music Concourse remain from this exposition, which was San Francisco's first world's fair.

2   In 1915, twenty million visitors attended this event, held in the Marina district. The Palace of Fine Arts is its lasting monument.

3   At this one-time-only affair on May 27, 1937, some 200,000 people paid a nickel to walk, run or rollerskate to Marin County and back.

4   In 1982, Jefferson Starship singer Grace Slick complied with the dress code of this only-in-San-Francisco gala event by wearing a nun's habit.

5   This three-day event in 1966 fused rock music, light shows and LSD, and spawned acid rock.

6   Held on the last Sunday of every June, what began as a political event has evolved into a street celebration involving a quarter of a million participants and spectators.

7   These Sunday summer concerts are free to the public. The performances run the gamut from New Orleans jazz to The City's symphony.

8   Violence at this 1969 Rolling Stones concert killed a man, and, some say, signaled the end of the Woodstock age as well.

9   He threw the party that ten thousand people attended at Pier 45 during the 1984 Democratic convention.

10   Approximately how many people ran in the 1985 Bay to Breakers?

PARTY HEARTY
Bay Area Celebrations

1   The Midwinter International Exposition of 1894, held in Golden
    Gate Park. While attending the Columbian Exposition of 1893 in
    Chicago, Michael H. de Young conceived the idea of this similar
    extravaganza for San Francisco.

2   The Panama Pacific International Exposition. This 635-acre
    exhibition was staged just nine years after the great earthquake,
    and commemorated the completion of the Panama Canal.

3   Opening day of the Golden Gate Bridge.

4   The Black and White Ball, begun in 1956 as a combination of The
    City's fiftieth anniversary celebration of surviving the earthquake
    and a symphony fundraiser. The 1985 ball hosted simultaneous
    parties in Davies Symphony Hall, the Opera House, Civic
    Auditorium, the Veterans Building, and City Hall rotunda.

5   The Trips Festival, held at Longshoreman's Hall.

6   The Lesbian Gay Freedom Day Parade.

7   Stern Grove concerts.

8   Altamont.

9   Willie Brown.

10 An estimated 75,000.

I CAUGHT THE CRABS
Fisherman's Wharf

1   When is the crab season in San Francisco Bay?

2   Who built what we now call Fisherman's Wharf?

3   On what pier is the museum ship *Balclutha*?

4   His son became mayor of San Francisco and he was president of the International Fish Company at Fisherman's Wharf.

5   Name the shopping center that is on the site of the Del Monte Fruit Company.

6   Which bar supposedly introduced Irish coffee to America?

7   This event takes place on the first Sunday after October 1.

8   When this restaurant opened in 1937, the baseball-playing owner was depicted in an electric sign.

9   The whaling industry flourished in San Francisco due to this historical event.

10   The cable car turnaround at Beach and Hyde streets is located in what park?

I CAUGHT THE CRABS
Fisherman's Wharf

1   Mid-November to the end of June.

2   Henry Meiggs. Meiggs built the wharf so ships carrying lumber would have a place to anchor.

3   Pier 43. The *Balclutha* was built in Scotland in 1886. It was exhibited at the 1939 world's fair on Treasure Island before being brought to Fisherman's Wharf.

4   Joseph Alioto.

5   The Cannery.

6   The Buena Vista Cafe at Beach and Hyde. Stanton Delaplane brought the recipe with him from a trip abroad.

7   The blessing of the fishing fleet.

8   Joe DiMaggio's Grotto.

9   The Gold Rush. Whaling ships were a quick means of transportation for the Eastern gold hunters. Once the ships reached California, the crews went out to sea capturing whales.

10   Victorian Park.

NEXT STOP, GRANT AVENUE
Chinatown

1   Name the dish that was created in 1878 during a San Francisco banquet for Li Hung-Chang, the first Chinese viceroy to visit our city.

2   What happens on the first day of the new moon after the sun enters Aquarius?

3   What are the Chinese Six Companies?

4   Who created a twelve-foot statue to commemorate this founder of the Chinese Republic, Dr. Sun Yat-sen?

5   What was unusual about Chinatown's phone service?

6   He headed a blackmailing society, Gi Sin Seer, and served five years in San Quentin.

7   This church was built using only volunteer labor.

8   Where is the Chinatown Gateway?

9   Chinese immigrants helped build this railroad associated with the Big Four.

10   This Chinatown waiter, sometimes thought to be a stand-up comedian, worked at Sam Wo's.

NEXT STOP, GRANT AVENUE
Chinatown

1   Chop suey, which means potpourri. At a lavish dinner the viceroy asked the waiter to bring him a simple dish of vegetables and meat. The waiter and cook concocted what we now know as chop suey.

2   Chinese New Year occurs between January 20 and February 20.

3   An affiliation of Chinese councils created in the 1850s to deal with the white community and also to solve problems in their own community. The various councils were formed by people either from a particular region in China or by groups having the same surname.

4   Beniamino Bufano.

5   Before direct dial went into effect, the callers would ask for the parties by name, not number. The twenty Chinese operators, needless to say, had terrific memories.

6   Quentin Fong Ching, known as Little Pete.

7   Buddha's Universal Church, completed in 1961.

8   Grant Avenue and Bush Street.

9   The Central Pacific. The first Chinese laborers were recruited from Chinatown. After 1865, labor crews came directly from China.

10   Edsel Ford Fong.

GEOGRAPHY

THE HILLS OF SAN FRANCISCO

1   Most people think San Francisco has seven hills. How many hills does it really have?

2   At an elevation of 938 feet, this is the highest peak in San Francisco.

3   This neighborhood was named after a no-longer-existing hilltop graveyard where seal traders were once buried.

4   In the late 1880s, this hill was known as Scotch Hill because of the Scottish immigrants who lived above the Union Iron Works.

5   In 1984, a ten-block area of the Mission became the fifth neighborhood to be granted special protection by the Landmarks Preservation Advisory Board. Name this section.

6   What is the shortest Muni bus route?

7   Early Spaniards called it Loma Alta. Name this hill.

8   What were steam paddies and what role did they play in shaping San Francisco's destiny?

9   Name the steepest street in San Francisco.

10   Postcard Row, a handsome line of Victorian houses often photographed with the modern downtown skyline contrasting in the background, is one of The City's most famous images. Yet many San Franciscans don't know where it is. Where is it?

THE HILLS OF SAN FRANCISCO

1   Forty-three. Alamo Heights, Anza Hill, Bernal Heights, Buena
     Vista Heights, Candlestick Point, Castro Hill, Cathedral Hill, City
     College Hill, College Hill, Corma Heights, Dolores Heights,
     Edgehill Heights, Excelsior Heights, Forest Hill, Gold Mine Hill,
     Holly Hill, Hunters Point Ridge, Irish Hill, Lafayette Heights,
     Larsen Peak, Laurel Hill, Lincoln Heights, Lone Mountain,
     McLaren Ridge, Merced Heights, Mount Davidson, Mount
     Olympus, Mount St. Joseph, Mount Sutro, Nob Hill, Pacific
     Heights, Parnassus Heights, Potrero Hill, Presidio Heights, Red
     Rock Hill, Rincon Hill, Russian Hill, Strawberry Hill, Sutro
     Heights, Telegraph Hill, Twin Peaks, University Mound,
     Washington Heights.

2   Mount Davidson. It was first dedicated as a city park on December
     20, 1929.

3   Russian Hill.

4   Potrero Hill.

5   Liberty Hill, bounded by Mission, Dolores, 22nd and 20th
     streets.

6   The 39 Coit, which runs only up and down Telegraph Hill.

7   Telegraph Hill.

8   Steam paddies were steam shovels, so nicknamed because "they
     could dig as much dirt as a team of Irish laborers." The speed with
     which these machines could level sand hills and create land fill
     greatly accelerated The City's expansion.

9   Filbert, between Hyde and Leavenworth, on Russian Hill. The
     grade is 31.5 degrees.

10   Postcard Row is on the eastern periphery of Alamo Square, on
     Steiner near Fulton.

ALL AROUND THE TOWN
Neighborhoods

1   How did Union Square get its name?

2   This district derived its name from the tradition of paying higher wages to police that worked in crime-ridden areas, thus enabling them to afford buying more expensive cuts of meat.

3   This neighborhood was named for its preponderance of dairy pastureland in the 1860s.

4   Where is Little Hollywood?

5   This neighborhood carries the name of the race track that once stood on its location.

6   What neighborhood possesses the repetitious rows of bungalows once known as the White Cliffs of Doelger?

7   In this part of The City, you can get caught breaking the speed limit and municipal court won't send you a summons.

8   Where is San Francisco's last inland sand dune?

9   Spanish explorers called this area Seashell Point. What is this neighborhood known as today?

10 Originally all land west of Van Ness, from the Marina to Market Street, was known by this name.

ALL AROUND THE TOWN
Neighborhoods

1   Union Square was named shortly before the Civil War when it was the site of pro-Union rallies.

2   The Tenderloin.

3   Cow Hollow. Most of San Francisco's milk came from here until the Board of Health ordered all cattle removed from the city limits in the 1880s.

4   Little Hollywood is the neighborhood bounded by Highway 101, Bayshore Boulevard and the San Mateo County line. This community derived its name from its architecture, whose Spanish roofs and arches reminded people of movieland homes of the 1920s and 1930s.

5   Ingleside, named after Ingleside Race Track (1885–1905). The old track's concrete sundial still remains at Entrada Court. Urbano Drive follows the contours of the raceway's mile-long oval.

6   The Sunset.

7   The Presidio. Instead of a traffic summons from the Hall of Justice, speeders get a federal court summons.

8   All that remains of the sandy expanse that was San Francisco's original environment is located between 37th and 41st avenues and Ortega and Quintara streets.

9   Hunters Point.

10   The Western Addition.

SNOB HILL

1 Once the Flood mansion, it now houses this exclusive men's club.

2 This Nob Hill hotel, built in the 1920s, has only 144 rooms.

3 After his death in 1893, his Nob Hill mansion was donated to The City, only to be destroyed in the 1906 earthquake.

4 The Top of the Mark bar was opened in 1939. What floor of the Mark Hopkins Hotel is it on?

5 While building his mansion on Nob Hill, which one of the Big Four erected a forty-foot spite fence?

6 Name the park on Nob Hill.

7 In what year was the Fairmont Hotel built?

8 Name the Big Four.

9 The doors of this Nob Hill building are a copy of the Ghiberti doors in Florence, Italy.

10 Nob Hill's appeal as a residential area was greatly increased with the popularity of this invention.

SNOB HILL

1   The Pacific Union Club. Silver King James Flood, a former saloon keeper, had a brass fence built to surround his mansion.

2   Huntington Hotel.

3   Leland Stanford.

4   Nineteenth floor.

5   Charles Crocker. Mr. Young, a neighbor of Crocker's on Sacramento Street, refused to sell Crocker a forty-foot lot for a reasonable sum of money. Rather than pay the inflated rate, Crocker built a tall fence between his property and Young's. Eventually Young gave in and sold his property to Crocker for a fair price.

6   Huntington Park.

7   It was built before the fire of 1906 and rebuilt in 1907. The hotel is located on the site of the first home on Nob Hill. In 1856, Dr. Arthur Hayne built his wife a home on this steep and then inaccessible hill.

8   Charles Crocker, Mark Hopkins, Collis P. Huntington and Leland Stanford.

9   Grace Cathedral. The famous bronze doors of the Baptistry in Florence were designed by Lorenzo Ghiberti in the fifteenth century. After World War II, a copy was made of the doors and later purchased by a donor for San Francisco's Episcopal cathedral.

10   The cable cars. Until a cable car line serviced the area, Nob Hill was all but inaccessible.

PASTA TO POETS
North Beach

1   This poet was arrested for publishing Allen Ginsberg's poem "Howl."

2   Where is the beach in North Beach?

3   This Italian restaurant has a plaque outside reading, "Rain or Shine, There's Always a Line."

4   What was the area around Washington Square called during the Gold Rush?

5   In 1955, this espresso coffeehouse was called the Piccolo.

6   Washington Square has two statues. One is the volunteer firemen's monument; name the other.

7   This North Beach nightclub claims to have the world's greatest female impersonators.

8   During the 1950s, comedian Mort Sahl got his start at this North Beach club.

9   This bar has an opera-only jukebox.

10   The door to Izzy Gomez' defunct Pacific Street saloon was on display in this North Beach bar.

PASTA TO POETS
North Beach

1   Lawrence Ferlinghetti, owner of City Lights.

2   It doesn't exist any longer. Land fill has covered it over. The bay originally came as far inland as Francisco and Taylor.

3   Little Joe's.

4   Little Chile, due to an influx of Chileans who came to California for gold and settled in North Beach before the Italians arrived. The square was originally called Spanish Lot in the 1840s when it was the potato patch of Juana Briones, Telegraph Hill's first resident.

5   Caffe Trieste.

6   Benjamin Franklin. The statue was donated by Dr. Henry D. Cogswell, a philanthropic dentist from the Gold Rush era.

7   Finocchio Club on Broadway.

8   The hungry i. While performing at the club, Sahl was given national attention for his daring comments on current events.

9   Tosca's.

10   Vesuvio's.

SOUTH OF THE SLOT
South of Market

1   This church's interior, facing Moscone Center, is decorated in the colors of a foreign country: green, white and gold.

2   What famous American author was born near the corner of Third and Brannan?

3   Which street is known for its gay leather bars?

4   This area took its name from ships of the Pacific Mail Steamship Company.

5   At Seals Stadium, formerly at 16th and Bryant, what was the Booze Cage?

6   Moscone Center was named for our slain mayor. What was the name originally intended for the convention center?

7   Where is San Francisco's other "crookedest street"?

8   In 1979, the name of this street was changed to Lapu Lapu, in recognition of the neighborhood's growing Filipino community. What was the former name?

9   This bar at Fifth and Howard has been popular with the newspaper crowd since World War II.

10   Prior to the 1870s, these two neighborhoods were considered The City's choicest residential areas.

SOUTH OF THE SLOT
South of Market

1   St. Patrick's on Mission Street. The colors are Ireland's, and there are stained-glass windows dedicated to each of her thirty-two counties.

2   Jack London. A Wells Fargo Bank branch now occupies the site of his home.

3   Folsom.

4   China Basin was named after the China Clippers that docked near there in the 1860s.

5   The Booze Cage was a row of field-level seats, running from first base to third base, behind home plate. This men-only section was enclosed by a metal fence, and served a shot of whiskey or two beers with the price of admission.

6   Yerba Buena Convention Center.

7   Vermont Street, near 22nd.

8   O'Doul Lane.

9   The M and M Tavern, named after Martin McVeigh and Mike Malloy.

10 Before the cable cars made the hilltops more accessible, many of the finest mansions were built at South Park and Rincon Hill.

McLAREN'S FOLLY
Golden Gate Park

1   Before he was appointed park superintendent in 1887, what was John McLaren's profession?

2   History tells us that this accident caused the sand dunes in Golden Gate Park to be able to support ground cover.

3   The Japanese Tea Garden was built for this event.

4   The authentic copy of a Dutch windmill, the North Windmill, was once used for what purpose?

5   Where is the annual Comedy Day Celebration held?

6   Recently restored, this attraction was originally at the world's fair on Treasure Island.

7   Where in the park can you find a tide pool?

8   Where are the park's two waterfalls located?

9   This area has flowers, shrubs and trees mentioned in "The Bard's" plays.

10   This park attraction was donated to The City by James Lick's estate in 1877.

McCLAREN'S FOLLY
Golden Gate Park

1   Landscape gardener. A statue of McLaren can be found in the rhododendron dell.

2   For many frustrating years nothing would grow in the dunes until a horse munching barley from a feed-bag thoughtfully spilled some barley in the sand. The barley mixed with lupine, and this winning combination made the park green.

3   The Midwinter International Exposition (1894–95). The fair made the park nationally famous.

4   Pumped water to irrigate the park.

5   At the Spreckels Temple of Music (also known as Spreckels Band Stand or the Music Pavilion).

6   The carousel.

7   Steinhart Aquarium.

8   Huntington Falls, built in 1893, flows down Strawberry Hill into Stow Lake. Rainbow Falls, dating from 1920, is near Prayerbook Cross.

9   Garden of Shakespeare's Flowers.

10   The Conservatory. It is a copy of the Kew Gardens Conservatory in England. Originally the Conservatory was to be erected on Lick's estate just outside San Jose.

THE POWER AND THE GLORY
Civic Center

1   Which is taller—San Francisco's City Hall or the Capitol in the District of Columbia?

2   In May of 1984, three hundred citizens attended a Board of Supervisors hearing while five thousand others gathered in City Hall's rotunda to follow the progress of a sometimes frivolous, sometimes bitter debate. Name the issue.

3   One of these is not an official sister city of San Francisco:
         a) Assisi, Italy.   b) Montreal, Canada.   c) Osaka, Japan.
         d) Sydney, Australia.   e) Taipei, Formosa.

4   What kind of vehicle is The City's official parade car?

5   Brooks Hall was named after The City's "no" man. Who was he?

6   What is San Francisco's official flower?

7   You can find the Nat Schmulowitz Collection of Wit and Humor here.

8   The signing of the United Nations Charter occurred here on June 26, 1945.

9   What U.S. president had his funeral at City Hall's rotunda?

10   This man was San Francisco's last alcalde and first mayor.

THE POWER AND THE GLORY
Civic Center

1   City Hall (308 feet). Mayor James Rolph, who dedicated the building, was fond of bragging that it was 16 feet, 2 ⅝ inches higher than the nation's Capitol. The correct figure is 11 feet, 7 inches.

2   The San Francisco official song controversy. While the supervisors watched Jeanette MacDonald perform on video tape, the crowds in the rotunda listened to the Gay Men's Chorus belt out "San Francisco," which was also sung in Mandarin by students from the Chinese American International School. The Hastings School of Law Rugby Club performed "I Left My Heart in San Francisco." What song won? "San Francisco" is now the official song; "I Left My Heart in San Francisco" is the official ballad.

3   Montreal, Canada.

4   A twelve-cylinder 1931 Lincoln touring car. Originally a police car, this vintage automobile has transported Douglas MacArthur, Admiral Chester W. Nimitz, Nikita Khrushchev and Bill Walsh, to name a few.

5   Thomas A. Brooks, San Francisco's chief administrative officer from 1941 to 1958. Brooks has been hailed as a model civil servant who could say "no" to politicians when necessary.

6   The dahlia.

7   The Special Collections Room of the San Francisco Public Library.

8   Herbst Theatre in the Veterans Building. During the United Nation's two-month long first session, high school students served as ushers and eight hundred Boy Scouts worked as messengers.

9   Warren G. Harding.

10   John Geary.

TOAST OF THE COAST
The Ocean

1   Below the Cliff House, this island is home to a tribe of sea lions.

2   This Marin County beach is the most popular in the Bay Area for tanning and swimming.

3   China Beach in Seacliff was renamed for this three-term mayor of San Francisco.

4   From 1885 until 1905, San Francisco was the center for this maritime activity.

5   These islands are populated mainly by millions of birds and hundreds of sea lions.

6   Name the two principal types of fog.

7   In the 1880s this Swedish sea captain had a fleet of ships that transported sugar and pineapple from the Hawaiian Islands to San Francisco.

8   What was the name of Sir Francis Drake's ship?

9   Recently, shifting currents have uncovered the timbers of a ship that was shipwrecked on Ocean Beach in 1875. Name the ship.

10   On permanent display here are anchors, figureheads, ship models and other relics of sailing ship days.

TOAST OF THE COAST
The Ocean

1   Seal Rocks. After the 1906 earthquake, the sea lions fled to the Farallon Islands and did not return for several years.

2   Stinson Beach.

3   James D. Phelan.

4   Whaling. The Pacific Coast was a prime area for hunting gray whales. Some whales were caught in the San Francisco Bay.

5   Farallon Islands. In 1909, the islands were declared a bird sanctuary.

6   Tule fog and white fog.

7   William Matson.

8   The *Golden Hinde*. In 1579 Drake sailed the coast of California but failed to find the fog-covered Golden Gate.

9   The *King Phillip*.

10   San Francisco Maritime Museum. The museum is housed in the Aquatic Park Casino, which was intended to be a haven for swimmers.

PEACOCK FEATHERS AND HOT TUBS
Marin County

1   In the 1880s, this Marin County town blossomed as a railway center.

2   Most of the land for this redwood forest was donated by Congressman William Kent and Elizabeth Thatcher Kent in 1908.

3   The residents of this oceanside town, twenty-seven miles north of San Francisco, rip down highway signs to discourage visitors.

4   Who designed Marin Civic Center?

5   Point Reyes is separated from the mainland by this geological curiosity.

6   Name the Marin complex of offices, apartments, condos, shops and restaurants that is on the site of a former rock quarry.

7   A Mill Valley landmark, it has an Indian name meaning "bay-mountain."

8   It's not all peacock feathers and hot tubs in Marin. Name the city that's a redeveloped World War II housing project for shipyard workers.

9   Each year runners complain of pulled tendons and twisted ankles after running the race on this Mount Tam trail.

10   In Spanish, the name of this Marin County town means "Little Grove of Willows."

PEACOCK FEATHERS AND HOT TUBS
Marin County

1   Tiburon. When a branch of the San Francisco and North Pacific Railroad was established between Tiburon and San Rafael, it was instrumental in helping Tiburon grow from a sleepy waterfront town.

2   Muir Woods.

3   Bolinas.

4   Frank Lloyd Wright in association with Aaron Green. The buildings were completed in the 1960s, after Wright's death. The Post Office Building is the only U.S. government commission that Wright ever received.

5   The San Andreas Fault, which runs down the middle of Tomales Bay.

6   Larkspur Landing.

7   Mount Tamalpais. Until 1930, Mount Tam had a twisting and turning railroad leading up the side of the mountain.

8   Marin City.

9   Dipsea.

10   Sausalito. The correct spelling is *Saucelito*, but a creative sign painter gave the town a new name when he painted the misspelled title in large letters over the ferry terminal at Fisherman's Wharf.

SOUR GRAPES
The Wine Country

1   Who was Napa Valley's first white settler?

2   Fort Ross, in Sonoma County, has what historical significance?

3   Who has been called the Father of California Viticulture?

4   California's first vineyards were planted not in the Napa-Sonoma area, but in this Southern California city.

5   This lake is the largest natural lake entirely within California.

6   Name California's mystery grape.

7   Why does Domaine Chandon call its bubbly "sparkling wine" instead of champagne?

8   Anthony Dicncr heads the International Correspondence of Corkscrew Addicts. He is known by another name as a famous Napa cellarmaster. What is his other name?

9   The World's Wrist-Wrestling Championship is held here each year.

10   In Napa Valley, you can get a great view from the top of this winery by taking an aerial tram.

SOUR GRAPES
The Wine Country

1   George Yount, for whom Yountville is named. Yount did a favor for
      General Vallejo, who was then based in Sonoma, and in exchange
      the Mexican government granted him an 11,000-acre tract of land
      comprising most of the valley.

2   It was a Russian outpost. From 1812 to 1841 the Russians had a
      trading post located on the Sonoma coast. The Russian-American
      Fur Company hunted otters, grew crops and established a trading
      colony.

3   Agoston Haraszthy, a Hungarian immigrant, planted about 86,000
      vines in the 1850s in Sonoma. He was the first to grow the
      European *vinafera* grapes in America.

4   San Diego. The first grapes were cultivated by Spanish
      missionaries in 1769.

5   Clear Lake.

6   Zinfandel. Though a European-type grape, its old-world origins
      have never been established.

7   The winery's parent company, Moet Chandon, is French and by
      French law, no wine produced outside of Champagne may be
      labeled "champagne."

8   Brother Timothy, cellarmaster of The Christian Brothers, Napa's
      largest winery.

9   Veterans Memorial Building in Petaluma.

10   Sterling Vineyards, located on a hilltop between St. Helena and
      Calistoga.

BERSERKELEY

1   By 1910, Berkeley's population had risen to over forty thousand as a result of this event.

2   This street had its name changed to Martin Luther King Junior Way in 1983.

3   Where is the "Gourmet Ghetto"?

4   The U.C. Memorial Stadium, which accommodates 76,000 people, was built atop what geological formation?

5   What two Berkeley grills are owned by former chefs of Chez Panisse?

6   Hanging Mickey Mouse gloves on its hands has been a campus ritual for each new generation. Name this U.C. landmark.

7   Who is the Bubble Lady?

8   Name the two best-known leaders of the Free Speech Movement.

9   Anyone who was anyone in the Berkeley protest scene drank coffee at this Telegraph Avenue cafe in the 1960s.

10   What renowned architect built a house with burlap sacks dipped in concrete in the Berkeley Hills?

BERSERKELEY

1   The influx of San Franciscans after the 1906 earthquake and fire.

2   Grove Street.

3   Shattuck Avenue, between Rose and Virginia streets, with its many boutiques and trendy restaurants.

4   The Hayward Fault.

5   Santa Fe Bar & Grill (Jeremiah Tower) and the Fourth Street Grill (Mark Miller).

6   The clock in Sather Tower, modeled after St. Mark's Campanile in Venice.

7   Julia Vinograd, author of twenty published books of poetry. She always wears a black and yellow hat and is called the Bubble Lady by street people because she, well, likes to blow bubbles.

8   Mario Savio and Jack Weinberg.

9   Caffe Mediterraneum.

10 Bernard Maybeck. The "Sack" House is located at 2711 Buena Vista Way. This construction material was dubbed "bubble-crete."

EAST OF EDEN
Oakland

1   Who said, "Oakland . . . there is no there, there . . ."?

2   How many Oaklanders died in the 1906 earthquake?
        a) 5.   b) 27.   c) 95.   d) none.

3   While doing research for his book *Hell's Angels*, this journalist was beaten up by members of the club's Oakland chapter.

4   Name the Alameda amusement park that was called the Coney Island of the West.

5   Famous singer Al Morris attended Oakland Tech. By what name is he more popularly known?

6   Today it is called Pill Hill because of the concentration of hospitals. What was it called originally?

7   When built in 1928, this was the largest theater west of Chicago.

8   Contra Costa Academy is the original name of this nationally renowned educational institution, which began in Oakland.

9   From 1962 to 1966, this was the home field of the Oakland Raiders.

10   This Oakland police chief later became San Francisco's police chief.

EAST OF EDEN
Oakland

1   Gertrude Stein, in *Everybody's Autobiography* (1937).

2   Approximately five. They were killed when a wall of the Empire Theatre collapsed on them.

3   Hunter S. Thompson.

4   Neptune Beach.

5   Tony Martin.

6   Academy Hill, because of the many private schools located in the vicinity. Among them were California Military Academy, Golden Gate Academy, and the Sackett School.

7   The Fox Oakland Theatre, 3200 seats.

8   U.C. Berkeley (1853). In 1859, a 160-acre tract of land was purchased north of Oakland to house the campus. To help pay for the land, lots were sold in a new community named Berkeley.

9   Frank Youell Field, near Laney College.

10 Charles R. Gain (Oakland Police Chief, 1967–73; San Francisco, 1976–80).

SOUTH OF THE BORDER
The Peninsula

1   Name the town that inspired Malvina Reynolds to write the song "Little Boxes on the Hillside."

2   During the 1800s, they roamed the Peninsula almost at will, and were more feared than earthquakes.

3   Kurt Machein, now a member of the physics department at Stanford, invented a process that is familiar to anyone who watches TV sports. What is it?

4   Name the San Bruno shopping center that is located on the former site of a race track and a World War II Japanese-American internment center.

5   When it was completed in 1929, the San Mateo-Hayward Bridge held what distinction?

6   Although she was a U.S. delegate to the United Nations (1969–72) and Ambassador to Ghana (1974–76), this Woodside resident is more famous for being Little Miss Marker (1934) and Rebecca of Sunnybrook Farm (1938).

7   In 1932, this airfield was renamed San Francisco Airport.

8   This major Peninsula thoroughfare was originally the eighteenth-century trail that linked California's chain of missions and pueblos.

9   In Colma, the dead outnumber the living by what ratio?

10   On January 18, 1911, aviator Eugene Ely took off from San Bruno to accomplish this aeronautical first.

SOUTH OF THE BORDER
The Peninsula

1   Daly City. "Little Boxes" was an ode to Daly City's builder, Henry Doelger. His mass-produced homes are in the hills west of Colma.

2   Grizzly bears. In 1859, a rancher caught one that weighed nearly eight hundred pounds.

3   Slow-motion replay. Machein developed it while president of a Peninsula firm called MVR. It was first used by CBS in 1965.

4   Tanforan Shopping Center. During the anxious months after Pearl Harbor, Tanforan Race Track became a temporary assembly center while 16 permanent internment centers were being built. Some 8000 Bay Area Japanese-Americans were kept here for 169 days.

5   It was the world's longest bridge, spanning nearly eight miles.

6   Shirley Temple Black. Ms. Black made her last feature film in 1949.

7   Mills Field, named for the estate it was built on.

8   El Camino Real.

9   More than 10 to 1. Colma's population is 730; there are over a million graves.

10 Ely made the first airplane landing on the deck of a ship. In the cockpit he wore bicycle tires as a makeshift life preserver. On the fourth attempt, he landed on the *U.S.S. Pennsylvania*, stopping five yards from the end of the deck.

A BODY OF LAND
COMPLETELY SURROUNDED BY WATER
Islands

1   The Ferry Building opened in what year?
    a) 1898.   b) 1863.   c)1907.

2   Where was the Golden Gate International Exposition of 1939 held?

3   Name the tiny island in San Pablo Bay whose lighthouse has been guiding sailors since 1873.

4   Angel Island is the largest island in San Francisco Bay. How large is it?
    a) 1 square mile.   b) 2 square miles.   c) 3 square miles.

5   In 1962, he ordered Alcatraz Prison to be closed.

6   This island, once an immigration station, is known as the Ellis Island of the West.

7   These islands can be yours for a mere $3.5 million.

8   These islands are legally part of the City and County of San Francisco.

9   The Moffitt House, on this exclusive residential island, was cut in half and moved from Broadway Street in San Francisco in 1962. Name the island.

10   The U.S. Army established a post on this island on December 19, 1866.

A BODY OF LAND
COMPLETELY SURROUNDED BY WATER
Islands

1   1898.

2   Treasure Island. With the outbreak of World War II the island
     became a U.S. Navy base.

3   East Brother.

4   One square mile.

5   Attorney General Robert F. Kennedy.

6   Angel Island. It was also a Nike missile base in the 1950s.

7   The Marin Islands, situated at the mouth of the San Rafael
     channel, are on the real estate listings.

8   The Farallon Islands are thirty-two miles from Point Lobos and
     have been part of San Francisco since 1872.

9   Belvedere.

10   Yerba Buena, which is now occupied by the U.S. Navy.

WHITE LINE FEVER
On the Road

1   This town likes to call itself The Artichoke Capital of the World.

2   Founded as a resort town in 1859, Calistoga's name is the hybrid of what two places?

3   Name Clint Eastwood's bar and restaurant in Carmel.

4   The City of San Francisco owns land near the entrance to this national park.

5   This town has a garlic festival every year.

6   From 1852 to 1853, this town in Solano County was the capital of California.

7   How old are the oldest redwood trees in Muir Woods?
    a) 200–300 years.   b) 400–500 years.   c) 600–700 years.
    d) over 1000 years.

8   This town has the world's longest-burning light bulb.

9   Swimmers flock to this bay in late summer, despite the fact that the San Andreas Fault runs right up the center.

10   This Bay Area city has the highest divorce rate in the state.

WHITE LINE FEVER
On the Road

1   Castroville.

2   California and Saratoga. In the nineteenth century, Saratoga, New York, was synonymous with horse racing and breeding. Shortly after founding Calistoga, wealthy businessman Sam Brannan began breeding horses, but a costly divorce settlement forced him to sell most of his Napa Valley holdings before Calistoga could become the Saratoga of the West.

3   The Hog's Breath.

4   Yosemite National Park. The area has cabins and picnic facilities. City residents get to enjoy the same natural splendor as Ahwahnee Hotel guests, at a fraction of the cost.

5   Gilroy.

6   Benicia.

7   According to the National Park Service, the oldest trees are over one thousand years old. The average age of Muir Woods' redwoods is four hundred to six hundred years.

8   Livermore. According to *The Guinness Book of Records*, the city's firehouse has a carbon filament bulb that has been working since 1901.

9   Tomales Bay.

10 San Jose, ranked 20th nationally, with 6.3 divorces per 1000 population. San Francisco-Oakland is ranked 34th, with 6.08 per 1000. Los Angeles is only 42nd with 5.42 per 1000. Las Vegas is first with 12.72 per 1000, according to the *Book of American City Rankings* (1983).

ON THE ROAD AGAIN

1   This Napa Valley mountain, just north of Calistoga, is actually an extinct volcano.

2   Both the San Francisco Seals and the Oakland Oaks baseball teams held their spring training in this Sonoma County town.

3   Name the South Lake Tahoe casino that was bombed in an extortion plot in 1980.

4   In this town, thirty-five miles south of San Francisco on Highway One, the local hardware store doubles as a tavern.

5   Sonoma County's Highway 116 is more commonly known by this name because of the particular kind of apple that grows along its route.

6   On what Monterey road will you find the Lone Cypress?

7   This strange house covers six acres and contains 160 rooms. The owner feared she would die if the construction on the house stopped.

8   Tennessee Valley Beach is one of the most popular outdoor attractions in Marin. Where did the name "Tennessee" come from?

9   Name the mock-Grecian structure near Crystal Springs Reservoir that bears a Biblical quotation from Isaiah.

10 Nestled in a forest of redwoods northeast of Sebastopol, this town is most famous for its three Italian restaurants: Fiori's, Negri's and the Union Hotel.

ON THE ROAD AGAIN

1   Mount St. Helena (elevation 4,344 feet).

2   Boyes Hot Springs.

3   Harvey's.

4   San Gregorio. In addition to having a bar, Peterson & Alsford's (1889) also serves as the town's coffee shop, bookstore, post office and gas station.

5   The Gravenstein Highway.

6   The Seventeen-Mile Drive.

7   The Winchester Mystery House, near San Jose.

8   The beach and the valley were named for the side-wheel steamer, the *Tennessee*, that ran aground there in 1853.

9   The Pulgas Water Temple. It was built to commemorate the connection of the Hetch Hetchy aquaduct with San Francisco's water system. The inscription reads: "I give waters in the wilderness and rivers in the desert, to give drink to my people."

10   Occidental. The town's restaurants are the legacy of the Italian woodcutters that came from Tuscany to work in the forests.

THE
GOOD LIFE

CULTURAL COLLAGE

1   Architecture critic Allan Temko called it a "fountain deposited by a dog with square intestines," and during the 1971 dedication ceremonies, its creator waded into the water and painted political graffiti on its base. Name the artwork and the sculptor.

2   What twentieth-century scientific and cultural phenomenon was spawned at the corner of Green and Sansome streets on September 7, 1927?

3   Name the satirical comedy revue that performed for eleven years at 622 Broadway.

4   What is the name of Francis Ford Coppola's motion picture production company?

5   This longshoreman-philosopher worked on the Embarcadero in the 1940s while writing *The True Believer, Thoughts on the Nature of Mass Movements* (1951).

6   This bodybuilder-actor began weightlifting at Oakland's Castlemont High School and, before becoming an international movie star, captured virtually every physical culture prize in the world.

7   Since 1949, this listener-sponsored radio station has featured live programs with Dylan Thomas, Robert Frost, William Carlos Williams and Robert Lowell, as well as regular programs by Alan Watts, Philip Elwood, Ralph Gleason, Kenneth Rexroth and Pauline Kael. Name the station.

8   This underground cartoonist created the Keep On Truckin' logo.

9   He created the "Running Fence" in Marin and Sonoma counties.

10   This famous opera star once cooked pasta at the California Culinary Academy. Name the singer.

CULTURAL COLLAGE

1 The Vaillancourt Fountain at Justin Herman Plaza near the Embarcadero. French Canadian sculptor Armand Vaillancourt painted "Quebec Libre" on his 710-ton, $310,000 work.

2 Television. Philo T. Farnsworth transmitted the first tele-electronic image, a bold black line painted on a glass slide, in his lab at 202 Green Street.

3 The Committee (1961–72). Some of its improvisational alumni were Howard Hesseman, Peter Bonerz, Gary Goodrow, Julie Payne, Jim Cranna, David Ogden Stiers, Nancy Fish, Bruce Mackey, Scott Beach, Rob Reiner, Katherine Ish, Barbara Bosson, Dan Barrows and Jessica Myerson.

4 Zoetrope Studios, 916 Kearny, formerly American Zoetrope.

5 Eric Hoffer.

6 Steve Reeves. After being crowned Mr. Pacific, Mr. America, Mr. World and Mr. Universe, he played mythological heroes in Italian movies. Some of his film credits include *David and Goliath*, *Goliath and the Barbarians* and *Hercules Unchained*.

7 Berkeley's KPFA-FM.

8 R. Crumb. This artist is also famous for cofounding Zap Comix, featuring Granola Guru, Mr. Natural.

9 Christo Javacheff.

10 Luciano Pavarotti. He had come to the academy's restaurant for dinner, but soon left his guests at table and spent the evening in the kitchen, cooking pasta with the student chefs.

WRITER'S CRAMP
Authors

1   The Silverado Museum in St. Helena is devoted to the life and works of this author.

2   In 1940, this author won the Pulitzer Prize for a play based on the real-life characters at Izzy Gomez's saloon at 848 Pacific Street. Name the author and the play.

3   Name the author whose memoirs, *What is Remembered*, include an account of the 1906 earthquake.

4   This poet wrote "Stanyan Street and Other Sorrows."

5   The author of *The Devil's Dictionary* met his death when he ran off to Mexico to join up with Pancho Villa.

6   This poet-playwright-singer-dancer-political activist was also the first black female fare collector on The City's Municipal Railway.

7   In Richard Brautigan's *The Abortion: An Historical Romance 1966*, an actual San Francisco branch library was used as a model for a fictional library that accepted any book brought in person by the author. Name the real branch library.

8   In November, 1978, after the Peoples Temple and the Moscone-Milk murders, the *San Francisco Examiner* commissioned a local poet to write a "poem of hope" for The City. Who was the author of "An Elegy to Dispel Gloom"?

9   From her Pacific Heights mansion, she turns out the novels that reputedly make her the most widely read female author in the world.

10 Mark Twain became friends with a city fireman he met in the Turkish baths at Montgomery Block, and later used the man's name for one of the author's most famous characters. Name this character.

WRITER'S CRAMP
Authors

1   Robert Louis Stevenson. In France he met and fell in love with an American woman, Fanny Osbourne. After her divorce, they were married on May 19, 1880, in San Francisco and honeymooned at the defunct Silverado Mine on Mount St. Helena.

2   William Saroyan refused the Pulitzer Prize for *The Time of Your Life*, citing the prize as too commercial.

3   Alice B. Toklas, a native San Franciscan.

4   Rod McKuen.

5   Ambrose Bierce. Besides being one of America's greatest satirists, Bierce was one of the founders of the Bohemian Club in 1872.

6   Maya Angelou.

7   Presidio Branch Library, 3150 Sacramento Street. Brautigan used the real address in the book and to this day, mail is received from inquiring authors.

8   Lawrence Ferlinghetti.

9   Danielle Steel, who counts among her best-sellers: *Passion's Promise, Once in a Lifetime* and *Going Home*.

10   Tom Sawyer, of Liberty Hose Company No. 2.

DON'T CALL IT FRESCO
Artists

1   Which artist created the statue "St. Francis of the Guns"?

2   The San Francisco Museum of Modern Art is not the only spot in Civic Center to exhibit contemporary works. One of The City's most important collections of paintings and sculptures by Bay Area artists is housed nearby. Where?

3   He won a Pulitzer Prize for taking the most famous photo of World War II, the flag raising at Iwo Jima.

4   Around 1930, Imogen Cunningham, Ansel Adams, Edward Weston, Willard Van Dyke, Paul Strand and other Bay Area photographers were representative of a move away from misty sentimentality toward literal sharpness. What was this group called?

5   For over forty years, until the late 1970s, this pile of stones and rubble near the De Young Museum was a familiar sight.

6   Founded by Lyle Tuttle, this museum contains the world's largest collection of a certain art form.

7   Locate the three Diego Rivera murals in The City.

8   This Marin County artist claims that the discreet charm of the local bourgeoisie provides fodder for his cartoon series, *The Now Society*.

9   Sculptor Al Sybrian created what famous Sausalito landmark?

10   At the Cow Palace in 1974, this group created "Media Burn," with a Cadillac smashing through a wall of burning television sets. Name this local art collective.

DON'T CALL IT FRESCO
Artists

1   Beniamino Bufano (1898–1970). Commissioned by Mayor Joseph Alioto after the assassinations of Martin Luther King, Jr. and Robert Kennedy, the statue was cast from guns turned in by San Franciscans.

2   Modesto Lanzone's restaurant in the Opera Plaza. One of The City's most respected art collectors, Modesto constantly changes the several hundred works on view at his restaurant.

3   Joe Rosenthal joined the *San Francisco Examiner* after World War II, and retired in 1983.

4   The f/64 group, named for the lens aperture that produces the sharpest focus and the greatest range.

5   The dismantled twelfth-century monastery of Santa Maria de Ovila. In the 1930s, William Randolph Hearst purchased the monastery and brought it here from Spain with the intent of having it rebuilt in Golden Gate Park. After years of civic inaction and a series of fires that destroyed the plans and the marked crates, the stones were eventually used in the Arboretum and to shore up Stow Lake.

6   The Tattoo Art Museum. Also exhibited are photographs of Mr. Tuttle himself, who is tattooed from neck to ankle.

7   San Francisco Art Institute (1931), Pacific Stock Exchange Lunch Club (1931) and City College of San Francisco (relocated from the 1939 Golden Gate International Exposition after the fair closed).

8   William Hamilton.

9   The Sausalito seal. The original was cast in concrete in 1957 and replaced by the current bronze version in 1966.

10   The Ant Farm.

YOU OUGHT TO BE IN PICTURES
The Movie Business in San Francisco

1   George Lucas (*Star Wars*) filmed much of this low-budget, science-fiction movie in the uncompleted BART tunnel under Market Street. Name the movie.

2   Where did Kim Novak jump into San Francisco Bay in Alfred Hitchcock's *Vertigo*?

3   Name the San Francisco films featuring Clint Eastwood as Dirty Harry. What is Dirty Harry's last name?

4   In the 1957 movie *Pal Joey*, Frank Sinatra tries to open a night-club while coping with Kim Novak and Rita Hayworth. Which San Francisco landmark was used as the club in the film?

5   Eddie Murphy and Nick Nolte smash up North Beach and other selected parts of town in this 1983 thriller, which was Murphy's movie debut.

6   In his 1967 film debut, Dustin Hoffman is spotted driving to Berkeley in the wrong direction: on the upper level of the Bay Bridge. Name the film.

7   The Bank of America building and Hyatt Regency Embarcadero combine to make one *very* large burning building in this action epic.

8   In the 1968 film *Bullitt*, how many hubcaps did the villain's car lose during the classic chase scene?

9   Gilbert M. Anderson and his partner, George K. Spoor, virtually invented the classic American western in Niles Canyon in the East Bay. What was the name of their production company?

10   In the final scene of this 1969 comedy, Groucho Marx sails on the bay wearing a Hare Krishna robe while smoking a joint.

YOU OUGHT TO BE IN PICTURES
The Movie Business in San Francisco

1   *THX 1138* (1971). This film was originally shot by Lucas as a student project at USC.

2   Fort Point. Also featured are Ernie's, Podesta Baldocchi (on Grant), Muir Woods, Mission Dolores, the Palace of Fine Arts, and the Palace of the Legion of Honor.

3   *Dirty Harry* (1971), *Magnum Force* (1972), *The Enforcer* (1976) and *Sudden Impact* (1983). Dirty Harry's last name is Callahan.

4   The Spreckels mansion, at 2080 Washington in Pacific Heights.

5   *48 Hours.*

6   *The Graduate.*

7   *The Towering Inferno* (1976).

8   Thanks to movie magic, the car lost five. Natives get a laugh when Steve McQueen's car turns off Geneva Avenue and is immediately on Russian Hill.

9   Essanay Studios.

10   *Skidoo.*

THE SEQUEL
The Movie Business in San Francisco II

1   America's Mercury astronauts got a "New York City" tickertape parade on Montgomery Street, then went to "Texas" at the Cow Palace in this 1983 film.

2   Pod people threatened to take over Telegraph Hill, Market Street and the Civic Center in this remake of a science-fiction movie, starring Donald Sutherland.

3   A killer kidnaps a girl from A. P. Giannini School, then gets captured on the pitcher's mound at Candlestick in this 1962 thriller, starring Glenn Ford and Lee Remick.

4   A chance encounter with a hobo in San Francisco helped Charlie Chaplin prepare for his starring role in this movie, made in the East Bay.

5   Union Square is the setting for much of this Francis Ford Coppola movie about a surveillance expert (Gene Hackman) who loses his professional detachment.

6   Walter Matthau chases a killer through The City, after an entire busload of Muni passengers were machine-gunned in Chinatown, in this 1972 film.

7   When the classic film *Greed* was made in San Francisco in 1923, the producer bought several houses and then removed their roofs and walls to shoot exteriors. What is his name?

8   In this 1947 film, Humphrey Bogart escapes from San Quentin and convalesces from plastic surgery in Lauren Bacall's apartment on Filbert and Montgomery.

9   Name the three Alfred Hitchcock movies filmed in the Bay Area.

10 What prominent San Franciscan played the pope in the movie *Foul Play*?

THE SEQUEL
The Movie Business in San Francisco II

1   *The Right Stuff.*

2   *Invasion of the Body Snatchers* (1978).

3   *Experiment in Terror.*

4   *The Tramp* (1915). Chaplin said that meeting the hobo showed the actor the joys and sorrows of life uncluttered with possessions.

5   *The Conversation* (1974). Robert Shields makes a cameo appearance displaying some of his classic Union Square mimicry. Local private detective Hal Lipset provided technical assistance.

6   *The Laughing Policeman.*

7   Erich Von Stroheim. The film was produced as a ten-hour epic, but later cut by the studio to less than two hours.

8   *Dark Passage.*

9   *Vertigo* (1958), San Francisco; *The Birds* (1963), Bodega Bay and Maiden Lane; and *Shadow of a Doubt* (1943), Santa Rosa.

10 Cyril Magnin. Grace Cathedral was used as the Vatican.

HOME VIDEO
San Francisco TV

1   This television police series (1954–60) filmed in The City starred
     Warner Anderson and Tom Tully as middle-aged San Francisco
     detectives.

2   Name the KPIX sportscaster who was only on the air thirteen
     weeks before he was replaced by Wayne Walker.

3   In the popular western *Have Gun, Will Travel*, what was the name
     of the fictitious San Francisco hotel that was Paladin's home?

4   In the late 1950s and early 1960s, this KGO show featured
     recorded rock music and live dancing in the studio.

5   Karl Malden and Michael Douglas co-starred in *Streets of San
     Francisco* from the show's beginning in 1972 to 1976. What actor
     replaced Douglas in the series' last year?

6   This woman caused quite a stir with her Hillsborough neighbors
     when she made a commercial for Coit Carpet Cleaners in her
     home.

7   This show portrayed a widow with two children who commuted
     every day from her home in Mill Valley to her job on a San
     Francisco magazine.

8   *Dialing for Dollars'* Pat McCormick once had a children's show in
     the Bay Area. What was its name?

9   Rock Hudson and Susan St. James starred in *McMillan and Wife*,
     playing The City's police commissioner and his wife. What San
     Francisco neighborhood did they live in?

10   In 1982, this television station showed a 3-D movie called *Gorilla
     at Large* and gave viewers gorilla-decorated 3-D glasses.

HOME VIDEO
San Francisco TV

1   *Lineup*. When it went into syndication, it was called *San Francisco Beat*.

2   Milt Kahn. Milt worked in public relations in Los Angeles, where he wrote a humorous newsletter called *Milt's Mirror*.

3   Hotel Carlton. The TV series was not filmed in San Francisco.

4   *Dick Stewart's Dance Party*.

5   Richard Hatch.

6   Kathryn Crosby.

7   *The Doris Day Show* (1968–73).

8   *The Charley and Humphrey Show*. The last broadcast was in 1973.

9   Sea Cliff.

10   KTZO Channel 20. The 1954 movie starred Lee J. Cobb, Anne Bancroft and Raymond Burr.

DON'T TOUCH THAT DIAL
San Francisco TV II

1   On this San Francisco children's show, which ended in 1967, the kids in the gallery were called the City Council.

2   This North Beach native began in the wholesale produce business immediately after graduating from Commerce High School. Today he gives advice to vegetable buyers on television and radio.

3   This high-flying action TV drama set in San Francisco starred Lloyd Bridges, and didn't last a year.

4   This Reagan administration cabinet member was once a Bay Area talk-show host. Name him.

5   After twenty-five years with KCBS radio, he became a newscaster on KPIX television in 1976.

6   On TV's *Dynasty*, the exterior views of the Carrington estate are filmed at this Bay Area mansion.

7   He played Jack Webb's partner on *Dragnet* for seven years. This actor also owned a San Francisco mortuary and a Ford dealership on Mission Street.

8   Before he was replaced in 1983, this weekend weatherman had used a toilet plunger, a mannequin's leg and a live snake as a weather map pointer.

9   Name the Fireman Chef on KPIX's *People Are Talking*.

10   In 1981, this was the only talk-variety show broadcast live five nights a week in the nation.

DON'T TOUCH THAT DIAL
San Francisco TV II

1   The *Mayor Art Show* starring Art Finley.

2   Joe Carcione.

3   *San Francisco International Airport* (October 1970–August 1971). Clu Gulagher co-starred.

4   Secretary of Defense Caspar Weinberger was the host of KQED's *Profile Bay Area* in the 1960s.

5   Dave McEllhatton.

6   The Filoli mansion in Woodside. Built for William Bourn by architect Willis Polk in 1916, its name stems from Bourn's personal motto: Fight, Love, Live.

7   Ben Alexander. Prior to his acting career, he had worked in the Los Angeles coroner's office.

8   Lloyd Lindsay Young. He now earns an estimated $250,000 a year in New York City.

9   Jim Neil.

10   Steve Jamison's *SFO*.

THE EARS HAVE IT
Local Radio

1   Name the radio soap opera about the Barbour family, which was first broadcast from San Francisco in 1932.

2   Which San Francisco radio station broadcasts the Forty Niner games live?

3   Name the pair of radio DJs whose regular guest list includes bumbling newsman O'Bradley O'Bradley, Jack Benny from Heaven, macho sportscaster Rick Raff and Lovely Little Linda Spindlemeyer.

4   This was the first radio station to broadcast play-by-play action of football between Western universities.

5   Radio station KSFO paid this late radio personality a handsome salary for not working.

6   Which FM personality was suspended for three days in 1982 when he let a call-in listener say an obscenity on the air waves?

7   In the 1970s KSAN was considered San Francisco's underground radio station. Who was responsible for making the station successful?

8   Name the morning DJ who is best known for his one-liners and crazy sound effects?

9   In the early 1960s Coyle and Sharp conducted their man-in-the-street interviews from the corner of this intersection.

10   Before he became a newstalk radio host, he was a full-time meteorologist in the U.S. Air Force.

THE EARS HAVE IT
Local Radio

1   *One Man's Family*. The show went on to be a national success, broadcast from Los Angeles coast to coast.

2   KCBS.

3   Frank Dill and Mike Cleary of KNBR. Dill is the straight man to Cleary's cast of comedic characters.

4   KPO.

5   Don Sherwood. They paid him in the five-figure range not to work for any competing radio stations.

6   Don Bleu of KYUU.

7   Tom Donahue.

8   Dr. Don Rose on KFRC

9   Powell and Market.

10   KGO's Jim Eason.

SAILOR ON HORSEBACK
Jack London

1   Jack London's mother's profession was:
    a) a spiritualist.   b) a letter writer for miners in the Gold
    Country.   c) a noted author.

2   Where was Jack London's first job after completing grade school?

3   Although he only attended for one semester, Jack London went to
    this university.

4   This book, published in 1903, about London's experiences in the
    Yukon brought him worldwide acclaim.

5   Jack's first wife was Bess Madden. Name his second wife.

6   At fifteen London became a pirate. What did he steal from the San
    Francisco Bay?

7   What book is the sequel to *Call of the Wild*?

8   Name the autobiographical treatise that describes London's
    addiction to alcohol.

9   How long did London spend in the Yukon?
    a) 1 year.   b) 6 years.   c) 10 years.

10 What is the name of London's famous ranch, located in the Valley
    of the Moon?

SAILOR ON HORSEBACK
Jack London

1   A spiritualist.

2   He worked full-time in a cannery in West Oakland for ten cents an hour.

3   U.C. Berkeley. Jack had completed only two years of high school. By studying at home he was able to pass the college entrance exam.

4   *Call of the Wild.* In one day his book sold ten thousand copies and went into its second printing.

5   Charmian Kittredge.

6   Oysters. On his sloop the *Razzle Dazzle* Jack raided privately owned oyster beds in the San Francisco Bay.

7   *White Fang.*

8   *John Barleycorn.*

9   One year.

10   Beauty Ranch. The ranch covered over three thousand acres and he spent vast sums of money making it a showplace.

I LOVE THE NIGHT LIFE
Black Tie Optional

1   While visiting San Francisco in 1967, this mink-clad international ballet star and her dancing partner were found hiding on a Haight-Ashbury rooftop during a drug bust. Name the two stars.

2   Name the San Francisco restaurant that is owned by the former White House chef to the John F. Kennedys.

3   The San Francisco Ballet was the first company in the United States to perform this ballet.

4   On Christmas Eve, in 1910, this famous singer sang at Lotta's Fountain to an estimated audience of 250,000.

5   In 1912, he conducted the premiere of Stravinsky's *Rite of Spring* for the Ballets Russes. Later he was conductor of the San Francisco Symphony for twenty-two years. Name the conductor.

6   Pulitzer Prize winner Sam Shepard has had more of his plays premiere at this theater than any other location.

7   What year was the first San Francisco Film Festival?

8   Closed in 1963, this was the oldest continually running jazz club on the West Coast.

9   When Carlo Cossutta was unable to perform *Otello* on the opening night of the San Francisco Opera's 1983 season, who flew across the country to become an operatic fireman to the rescue?

10   Closed in 1975, it was San Francisco's longest-running dramatic stage play.

I LOVE THE NIGHT LIFE
Black Tie Optional

1   Dame Margot Fonteyn and Rudolf Nureyev. They had just
     performed the somewhat psychedelic *Paradise Lost* with the Royal
     Ballet at the Opera House before going to a hippie party. Both
     spent four hours in jail, but charges were dropped against them the
     next day.

2   Rene Verdon's Le Trianon on O'Farrell.

3   *The Nutcracker*, in 1944.

4   Luisa Tetrazzini.

5   Pierre Monteux, conductor and musical director of the San
     Francisco Symphony from 1935 to 1957. He also conducted the
     Metropolitan Opera, the Boston Symphony and in 1960 was
     appointed permanent conductor of the London Symphony.

6   The Magic Theatre at Fort Mason.

7   1957.

8   The Blackhawk. Dave Brubeck, Cal Tjader and Thelonius Monk
     recorded albums there.

9   Placido Domingo.

10   *One Flew Over the Cuckoo's Nest*. This Dale Wasserman
     adaptation of Ken Kesey's novel ran at the Little Fox Theatre for
     five years.

FUN CITY
Night Life II

1   During her visit to San Francisco in 1983, Queen Elizabeth II ate in a restaurant for the first time in her life. Name the restaurant.

2   For years this club was famous for its live "girl in the fishbowl." Name the club.

3   Before he retired in 1984, he had been the orchestra leader for thirty-six years at the Fairmont Hotel's Venetian Room.

4   In the 1930s this cafe was the center of bohemian society in San Francisco, and after World War II evolved into what many consider The City's first gay bar.

5   This is the only place where you can bowl all night in San Francisco.

6   Friday evening magic shows are a tradition at this hostelry near Lafayette Park.

7   In 1984 and 1985, he was master of ceremonies for the BAMMIES (Bay Area Music Awards).

8   Lord Jim's, at Broadway and Polk, is the former location of what other famous San Francisco bar?

9   This jazz band played at the Dawn Club on Annie Street in 1940 with Bob Scobey on trumpet, Clancy Hayes on banjo, Turk Murphy on trombone and Wally Rose on piano. Who was the trumpet-playing bandleader?

10   In the 1960s, the future of the Orpheum Theatre at Eighth and Market appeared to be doomed. What event occurred in 1970 to change the course of the Orpheum's history?

FUN CITY
Night Life II

1   Trader Vic's.

2   Bimbo's 365 Club, originally on Market Street. The girl looked like she actually was in the fish bowl, but the trick was done with mirrors. Bimbo's later moved to Columbus Avenue and the 365 Club is now a banquet hall.

3   Ernie Hecksher.

4   The Black Cat, 710 Montgomery.

5   Japantown Bowl at Post and Webster, but only on Friday and Saturday nights.

6   The Mansion Hotel, 2220 Sacramento.

7   Dick Bright.

8   Henry Africa's.

9   Lu Watters.

10   The rock musical *Hair* opened and the theater once again had enormous crowds reminiscent of its past.

BETTER READ THAN DEAD
The Press

1   Name San Francisco's first newspaper.

2   Which headline actually appeared in the *San Francisco Chronicle*?
      a) "Blue Skies Unless It's Cloudy."
      b) "Di Fi's Do Gets Undone."   c) "Man Bites Dog."

3   What is the name of the first San Francisco newspaper printed after the 1906 earthquake?

4   Until recently, this newspaper's masthead bore the slogan, "Monarch of the Dailies."

5   This Marin County weekly (circulation 3,500) won a Pulitzer Prize in 1979.

6   Mark Twain, Bret Harte and Ambrose Bierce all worked for this newspaper at the same time.

7   What was the name of Francis Ford Coppola's ill-fated magazine?

8   Mark Powelson and Warren Sharpe, editor and managing editor of *San Francisco Focus*, formerly held the same positions in what publication?

9   Now a respectable national magazine based in New York City, this former San Francisco hippie tabloid took its name from a Muddy Waters song performed on Bob Dylan's first rock record.

10   The *San Francisco Chronicle* did not start out as a newspaper. What is its origin?

BETTER READ THAN DEAD
The Press

1   *The California Star*, founded by Sam Brannan in 1847. It ceased publication in 1849 when its printers took off for the Gold Rush.

2   "Blue Skies Unless It's Cloudy" (May 29, 1971).

3   The *Call-Chronicle-Examiner*, published the day after the quake. With the presses of all three city dailies in ruins, this paper was a collaborative effort by the news staffs, and printed on a borrowed press in Oakland. Within a week, all papers returned to independent operation.

4   The *San Francisco Examiner*. The slogan was William Randolph Hearst's idea.

5   The *Point Reyes Light*.

6   The *Call* in 1864.

7   *City of San Francisco Magazine* (1973–75).

8   *The Berkeley Barb*.

9   *Rolling Stone*, founded by jazz columnist Ralph Gleason and Jann Wenner on October 2, 1967. Its premiere issue featured a photo spread of a police raid of the Grateful Dead's house on Ashbury Street.

10   It began as the *Dramatic Chronicle*, a theater sheet. In 1868, it became a daily newspaper.

BEACH BLANKET BABYLON GOES TRIVIAL

1   One of these is *not* a title of the Beach Blanket Babylon
     Productions:
     a) *Beach Blanket Babylon Goes to the Stars.*
     b) *Beach Blanket Babylon Goes to the Movies.*
     c) *Beach Blanket Babylon Goes to the Beach.*
     d) *Beach Blanket Babylon Goes to the Prom.*

2   On February 6, 1985, he attended his four hundredth
     performance of Beach Blanket Babylon.

3   This former star of Beach Blanket was a regular on the ill-fated
     television revival of *Laugh-In.*

4   Although she's never appeared in the cast, she is featured in the
     poster for *Beach Blanket Babylon Goes to the Stars.*

5   Who was feted at Davies Hall by the Beach Blanket Babylon cast in
     1983?

6   For their seventh anniversary show Beach Blanket Babylon went to
     the beach. Who was their one-night-only star for the show?

7   Which president invited Beach Blanket to perform on the south
     lawn of the White House?

8   He is BBB's producer, director and designer.

9   This popular character sang her Beach Blanket swan song on
     December 31, 1984.

10   What two songs always end the Beach Blanket show?

BEACH BLANKET BABYLON GOES TRIVIAL

1   *Beach Blanket Babylon Goes to the Movies.*

2   Cyril Magnin.

3   Nancy Bleiweiss.

4   Charlotte Mailliard.

5   Queen Elizabeth II. At the finale of the show a model appeared wearing a giant hat with a reproduction of Buckingham Palace and Big Ben on top. The clock face opened to display pictures of the Queen, Prince Philip, Prince Charles and Princess Diana.

6   Ex-Mouseketeer Annette Funicello.

7   In 1981, President Reagan extended the cast of Beach Blanket an invitation to do their thing for both houses of Congress. Some Democrats objected to the performance when it was discovered that the production was nonunion. Beach Blanket never made it to the White House nor to the bargaining table.

8   Steve Silver.

9   Snow White.

10   "Happy Trails to You" and "San Francisco."

SHOPPING SPREE

1   Enrico Caruso had floral arrangements for his Palace Hotel suite
     supplied by this florist.

2   The first of these clothing stores to sell pith helmets, safari shirts
     and bush hats opened its doors in Mill Valley.

3   Now it's a chic Post Street store, but in 1861 the owner sold frames
     and mirrors to local bars and bordellos.

4   When this complex was first built, owner Leonard Martin had
     twelve trained penguins entertaining the shoppers.

5   Over one hundred years ago this family-owned business was selling
     notions and yard goods.

6   Richard Thalheimer distributed his company's first catalog
     featuring gadgets for executives in 1979. Name the company.

7   In 1876, this Union Square store specialized in lace and baby
     clothes.

8   Williams-Sonoma, the Bay Area-based chain of gourmet cookware
     shops, has twenty-six stores in eleven states. What was founder
     Chuck Williams' first retail enterprise?

9   Name San Francisco's first department store.

10   Originally this San Francisco clothing manufacturer was called
     Plain Jane.

SHOPPING SPREE

1   Podesta Baldocchi, originally called the Venice Floral Company. The florist shop is noted for the elaborate decorations it has on display during the Christmas season, a tradition that began in 1944.

2   Banana Republic.

3   Gump's.

4   The Cannery.

5   Livingston's.

6   The Sharper Image. Thalheimer got the money to finance the San Francisco-based company by placing a $200 ad in *Runner's World* magazine for a sports watch. The ad reaped a hefty $300,000 in sales.

7   I. Magnin.

8   A hardware store in Sonoma. Williams had been in the real-estate development business until 1956, when he renovated a building in Sonoma that housed a hardware store, which he decided to operate himself, adding lines of cookware. In 1958, he moved the store to San Francisco and the rest is retail history.

9   The City of Paris, built in 1850 by the Verdier family.

10   Esprit. Their factory in the Potrero District produces sportswear that brings in $800 million in annual sales.

B.A.R.F.
Bar and Restaurant Facts

1   Name San Francisco's two revolving restaurants.

2   Name the North Beach restaurant whose softball team received national publicity in 1979 by playing games in France and England.

3   This chef is so adamant about using only American foods that he refuses to allow imported cheeses in his kitchen. Yet the food is served on imported Wedgwood china. Name the restaurant.

4   Sam Spade ate here in Dashiell Hammett's novel, *The Maltese Falcon*.

5   Name Boz Scaggs' bar and restaurant.

6   The decor of this famous hamburger emporium includes an extensive White House presidential plate collection.

7   Until 1970, this German restaurant refused to serve women before 1:30 pm.

8   In 1978, this old waterfront cafe was literally lifted in its entirety to the second floor of Pier 39.

9   This restaurant has been known by generations of San Franciscans for its eighteen tiny pancakes per order.

10   The band in this place floats on a raft and is interrupted every twenty minutes by an indoor tropical storm, complete with rain and thunder.

B.A.R.F.
Bar and Restaurant Facts

1   The Crown Room of the Fairmont Hotel and the Equinox at the Hyatt Regency.

2   The Washington Square Bar & Grill.

3   Campton Place on Stockton, run by executive chef Bradley Ogden.

4   John's Grill on Ellis. A favorite of the author's, the restaurant now has a Dashiell Hammett Room.

5   The Blue Light Cafe on Union Street.

6   Bill's Place on Clement.

7   Schroeder's Cafe on Front Street. Opened in 1893, it would not serve women at all until 1935.

8   The Eagle Cafe. Nothing much has changed in this haven for seamen and longshoremen, except the view through the window.

9   Sears Fine Foods on Powell.

10 The Tonga Room in the Fairmont Hotel. This night spot was originally an indoor swimming pool and was used as such until 1945.

SECOND HELPINGS
More Bar and Restaurant Facts

1   Who said: "California cuisine has come a long way since the 1930s, when food fads here were cinnamon toast and artichokes"?

2   Joyce Goldstein was chef at Chez Panisse until she opened Square One in 1984. Who replaced her at Chez Panisse?

3   This restaurant started during the Gold Rush as a wharfside tent where Yugoslavian immigrants dispensed coffee to arriving forty-niners.

4   What famous salad dressing was created by a chef at the Palace Hotel?

5   This North Beach Italian restaurant is named after a Chinese cook.

6   When it opened in 1939, this famous bar had a "weeper's corner."

7   Where was Trader Vic Bergeron's first restaurant?

8   This bar had a policy of asking men to leave if management judged their hair to be too long.

9   This restaurant changed its name because its patrons mispronounced the actual name: Poulet d'Or.

10   Contributing to the ambience of this popular bar are: an autographed picture of Hopalong Cassidy, an unautographed picture of Richard Nixon with the Lone Ranger, and the old neon sign from Morey's Bar.

SECOND HELPINGS
More Bar and Restaurant Facts

1   Julia Child, during a talk at the California Culinary Academy in 1981.

2   Paul Bertolli. A former music student at U.C. Berkeley, he had cooked at Fourth Street Grill for two years and worked in restaurants in Florence, Italy, for a year before joining the Chez Panisse staff in 1982.

3   Tadich Grill, The City's oldest restaurant. Though owners have changed over the years, they have always been Yugoslavian.

4   Green goddess dressing.

5   Tommaso's on Kearny. Formerly called Lupo's Pizzeria, it is now named after the Lupos' Chinese chef, the late Tommy Chin.

6   Top of the Mark in the Mark Hopkins Hotel. Weeper's corner derived its name from departing military men and their loved ones. During World War II, this establishment called its bartenders "bombardiers," and any serviceman in uniform got his first drink free.

7   Hinky Dink's in Oakland.

8   The Redwood Room at the Clift Hotel. Before this policy ended about 1978, some of the personae non gratae included actors Michael Douglas and Anthony Geary, and members of the Rolling Stones.

9   The Old Poodle Dog, now in its fifth location at the Crocker Galleria.

10   Perry's on Union Street.

SPORTS

PEOPLE IN SPORTS

1   Cedrick Hardman was the first player to sign with this Oakland team.

2   Only two people have ever played in both the World Series and the Rose Bowl. One was Jackie Jensen of U.C. Berkeley. Name the other.

3   During the 1972 Olympics, this Terra Linda swimmer lost his gold medal after urine tests revealed his prescribed asthma medication contained a banned drug. Name the swimmer.

4   What jockey "returned from the dead" at Bay Meadows on May 8, 1936?

5   He won the San Francisco city golf championship in 1950 at age eighteen, then won it again in 1953 and 1956.

6   Name the Bay Area sportscaster who is a former linebacker with the Detroit Lions.

7   What local baseball player holds the record for hitting into double plays in the World Series?

8   This team was once owned by Charlie Finley and then by Mel Swig. Name the team.

9   Who was the Mad Bomber?

10 Name the oldest active professional athlete in the Bay Area.

PEOPLE IN SPORTS

1   The Oakland Invaders football team.

2   Chuck Essegian of Stanford.

3   Rick DeMont. This sixteen-year-old swimmer had complied with regulations by listing his prescription, containing ephedrine, on his pre-Olympic forms, but U.S. team officials failed to pass this information on to the international committee. Had he been advised not to take this medication during competition, his victory in the 400-meter freestyle events would have been valid.

4   Ralph Neves. Doctors pronounced him dead at the hospital where he had been rushed after his horse tripped and threw him headfirst into the rail. Already covered with a sheet, Neves suddenly woke up and, remembering he had another race that day, took a taxi back to the track. When he arrived, his wife was being consoled by the track president and the jockeys were taking up a collection for his funeral wreath.

5   Ken Venturi, who went on to win fourteen PGA championships during his professional career.

6   Wayne Walker of KPIX.

7   Joe DiMaggio (seven times).

8   The California Seals ice hockey team.

9   Oakland Raider quarterback Daryle Lamonica.

10   Ann Calvello skated with the original Bay Bombers in 1954 and has skated every year since. A resident of San Mateo, she is currently with the Southern Jolters roller derby team.

THE SWEET SCIENCE
Boxing

1   This former member of the Hayward Boy's Club won the world
     heavyweight boxing title in 1973.

2   James "Gentleman Jim" Corbett became heavyweight champion
     by knocking out John L. Sullivan in 1892, but this San Francisco
     native's first famous victory was knocking out Joe Choynski in the
     twenty-seventh round in 1889. Where was the fight held?

3   Name the San Franciscan who fought for the world heavyweight
     championship on October 14, 1949, at the Cow Palace.

4   Who was the unusual referee in the heavyweight boxing match
     held at the Mechanic's Pavilion in San Francisco on December 2,
     1896?

5   Managed by San Francisco's Billy Newman, he was the 1953
     middleweight world boxing champion.

6   Retired in 1976, he was the *Examiner*'s boxing writer for fifty-two
     years.

7   On May 19, 1940, the Pride of the Mission defeated Verne Bybee,
     the Brisbane Buzzsaw in a lightweight bout at Civic Auditorium.
     Who was this victorious third-generation San Franciscan?

8   Name the San Franciscan who held the bantamweight boxing title
     for only two months in the mid-1930s.

9   Boxer Max Baer was charged with manslaughter when his
     opponent died after a pro match in San Francisco. Name the
     fighter who died.

10   Since 1924, Newman's Gym in the Tenderloin has been The City's
     professional boxing mecca. Before the fighters took over, what was
     this place?

THE SWEET SCIENCE
Boxing

1   George Foreman. He also won an Olympic gold medal in Mexico City in 1968.

2   Because boxing was illegal on land, Corbett fought Choynski on a grain barge anchored off Benicia. Spectators watched the grueling bare-knuckle match from bleachers on the shore and from boats.

3   Pat Valentino. He lost to Ezzard Charles.

4   Ex-gunfighter Wyatt Earp, former marshal of Tombstone and Dodge City. Earp entered the pavilion wearing a loaded revolver, but was disarmed by city police.

5   Bobo Olson.

6   Eddie Muller.

7   Ray Lunny.

8   Tony Marino.

9   Frankie Campbell. He died August 26, 1930.

10   The ballroom of the Cadillac Hotel. Boxers who have trained at Newman's include Jim Braddock, Jack Dempsey, Joe Louis, Muhammad Ali, Ezzard Charles, Sugar Ray Robinson and Rocky Marciano.

THEY'RE OFF AND RUNNING
Racing

1   On September 7, 1975, this apprentice jockey won six races in one day, something no other apprentice had accomplished. Name the jockey.

2   New Zealander Rod Dixon won the Bay to Breakers in 1982 and 1983. In what unique capacity did he run in the 1985 race?

3   This horse died in 1977 at the Green Oaks Stables in Pleasanton at age twenty-two. He ran in the Kentucky Derby in 1958, the year Tim Tam won. What was his name?

4   The first time this race was run, over seventy years ago, it had only two participants. The race celebrated The City's recovery after the 1906 earthquake.

5   This Hall of Fame jockey won his first race at Tanforan in 1931, and was ranked number one until Willie Shoemaker passed his record of 6,023 wins.

6   What annual event was started by a group known as PAMAKIDS?

7   Name the female jockey who was in a coma for a week after taking a spill at Golden Gate Fields in June, 1982.

8   After the Bay to Breakers, this is San Francisco's second oldest race.

9   Trained by Stanford graduate Ed Gregson, this horse won the 1982 Kentucky Derby.

10   This one-time-only race covered 480 miles.

THEY'RE OFF AND RUNNING
Racing

1   Bay Area jockey Russell Baze, who races at both Bay Meadows and Golden Gate Fields.

2   Unable to compete seriously because of a strained Achilles tendon, Dixon formed a team with blind runner Tom Sullivan, running as his "eyes."

3   Silky Sullivan.

4   The Bay to Breakers.

5   Johnny Longden.

6   The San Francisco Marathon. It was started by a small group of families (hence the name pa, ma and the kids) that ran around Lake Merced and organized races in The City. The Marathon now attracts over ten thousand runners annually from all over the world.

7   Mary Bacon.

8   The Statuto, first run in 1919, is sponsored by the San Francisco Italian Athletic Club.

9   Gato Del Sol.

10   The Great Redwood Highway Indian Marathon. The race was a publicity stunt to promote the scenic attractions between San Francisco and Oregon. It was open to American Indian participants only.

TAKE ME OUT TO THE BALL GAME

1   The San Francisco Seals sold this third baseman to the Chicago White Sox for $100,000 in 1922.

2   This Bay Area sports figure won Most Valuable Player in both the American and National leagues.

3   This Baseball Hall of Famer pitched for Richmond High School and was signed with the San Francisco Seals at age seventeen.

4   He led the National League in stolen bases four years in a row: 1956, 1957, 1958 and 1959.

5   Born in San Francisco, this Baseball Hall of Famer managed the Red Sox to a pennant in 1945.

6   Who were the San Francisco Eagles?

7   Which San Francisco pub was home to the Chicago Cubs fans during the 1984 season?

8   Who was the "Mayor of Powell Street"?

9   We all know the baseball-playing Seals, but name San Francisco's other Pacific Coast League team.

10   In 1929 this Seals baseball player set a home run record of 51 for the season.

TAKE ME OUT TO THE BALL GAME

1   Willie Kamm.

2   Former Giants manager Frank Robinson (American League 1966, Baltimore Orioles; National League 1961, Cincinnati Reds).

3   Vernon "Lefty" Gomez, who went on to play for the New York Yankees from 1930 until 1942.

4   Willie Mays of the Giants.

5   Joe Cronin.

6   The Eagles were the first organized baseball team in San Francisco, established in 1859.

7   Pat O'Shea's Mad Hatter at Geary and Third.

8   Seals baseball great Lefty O'Doul.

9   The Mission Reds. The team played from 1926 to 1937 and shared Recreation Park with the Seals as their home field.

10 Gus Suhr.

GOOD SPORTS FROM THE EAST BAY

1   Name the team Billy Martin played with before being signed by the New York Yankees in 1949.

2   In 1984, this Oakland team claimed to be the "nicest guys in the world."

3   Shep Messing was the goalie for this short-lived Oakland soccer team.

4   A sports first occurred during the Oakland A's and the New York Yankees playoff game on October 15, 1981. What was it?

5   What do John Ralston, Chuck Hutchison and Charlie Sumner have in common?

6   This team's all-time attendance record was set on July 4, 1971, at the Oakland Coliseum when 34,418 fans were in attendance.

7   This Oakland-born baseball player won the 1938 batting title while with the Cincinnati Reds.

8   This tennis champion and honors graduate from U.C. Berkeley was known as Little Miss Poker Face because of her serious demeanor on the court.

9   Owned by El Cerrito businessmen Richard Granzella and Lewis Figone, this race horse was named after the Oakland A's manager.

10   Name the Oakland tennis great who won the U.S. and Wimbledon men's championships in 1937.

GOOD SPORTS FROM THE EAST BAY

1   The Oakland Oaks.

2   The Oakland Invaders football team. With a win-loss record of 7–11 that year, maybe they took their advertising slogan seriously.

3   The Oakland Stompers.

4   Cheerleader Krazy George had the fans in the Oakland Coliseum perform the first "human wave."

5   They have all been the head coach for the Oakland Invaders football team.

6   San Francisco Bay Bombers roller derby team.

7   Ernie Lombardi.

8   Helen Wills Moody Roark, considered one of the greatest woman tennis players in the world, learned to play at the Berkeley Tennis Club. She won eight Wimbledons from 1927 to 1938 and seven U.S. singles titles from 1923 to 1931.

9   Billy Ball.

10   Don Budge.

ODDS AND ENDS

1   After a five-hour battle near Benicia on July 9, 1983, Joey Pallotta landed the largest fresh-water fish ever caught with a fishing rod in California. How old was this 468-pound white sturgeon?
     a) 25 years.   b) 50 years.   c) 75 years.   d) 100 years.

2   In 1939, this Sunset District native won both the British and U.S. singles and doubles titles.

3   Who was Clementine?

4   Formed in 1977, this was San Francisco's minor league ice hockey team.

5   Name the two San Francisco sportswriters who fought a fist fight in Golden Gate Park.

6   What was the former name of the Cleveland Barons?

7   Name the swimmer who won two gold medals in the 1949 Olympics.

8   This is the second-oldest yacht club in the United States.

9   Name the conference the Forty Niners played in when they were first formed as a team in 1946.

10   A thirty-year veteran of the San Francisco Bay Bombers roller derby team, she is known as the "Blonde Bombshell."

ODDS AND ENDS

1   An estimated 100 years old.

2   Alice Marble.

3   The burro mascot for the Forty Niners from 1954 to 1966.

4   The San Francisco Shamrocks.

5   The *Examiner*'s Prescott Sullivan and the *News'* Tom Laird. Legend has it that Laird, piqued by a Sullivan remark, challenged him to a fight and timed it so the sun would be in Sullivan's eyes. Sullivan was felled early, then went back to the office and wrote a column about it. This column is considered one of his best.

6   The old California Seals ice hockey team became the Barons in July, 1976.

7   Ann Cuneo, a San Francisco native.

8   The San Francisco Yacht Club in Belvedere, Marin County. The club was opened in 1869.

9   The All-American Conference.

10   Joan Weston.

FORTY NINER FEVER

1 What was the final score in Super Bowl XVI?

2 In 1956, he was the highest-paid professional in football.

3 Before turning professional, he coached Santa Clara's upset Sugar Bowl victories.

4 Roger Craig made three touchdowns in Super Bowl XIX, but which player scored the first touchdown for the Niners?

5 When the Forty Niners were first formed as a team in 1946, who did their play-by-play on radio and television?

6 What team was Bill Walsh with before taking over as head coach for the Forty Niners in 1979?

7 Quarterback John Brodie was injured in the fifth game of the 1972 season and did not play again until the last quarter of the last game. Who replaced him?

8 Name the Forty Niner who played fourteen seasons without missing a game.

9 Who made the first touchdown for the Forty Niners in Super Bowl XVI?

10 Name the Forty Niner who was the first man ever to gain more than one thousand yards in two seasons.

FORTY NINER FEVER

1   San Francisco 26, Cincinnati 21.

2   Y. A. Tittle, quarterback, made a record $21,000 that year.

3   Buck Shaw, the Forty Niners' first head coach.

4   Carl Monroe. He also made the first touchdown of the 1984 season for the Niners and didn't make another until the Super Bowl.

5   Bob Fouts.

6   The Cincinnati Bengals. Walsh was their offensive coordinator for eight years and was very disappointed when he wasn't offered the head coach position.

7   Steve Spurrier replaced Brodie for nine games.

8   Leo Nomellini, who was inducted into the San Francisco Sports Hall of Fame on February 21, 1985.

9   Joe Montana. He was voted MVP in that game.

10   Joe "Jet" Perry. He accomplished that feat in 1953 and 1954.

MORE FORTY NINER FEVER

1   He was the Forty Niners' first quarterback and later he became their coach.

2   In the famous "Alley-Oop" pass who was Y. A. Tittle's receiver?

3   When O. J. Simpson injured his shoulder in 1978, who replaced him as running back?

4   Name the coach who first used the shotgun attack.

5   In 1970, he was named the NFL's Player of the Year.

6   Forty Niner owner Tony Morabito had a heart attack and died during a home game on October 27, 1957. The Niners were losing 17 to 7 and came back to win the game. What team were they playing?

7   Fresh from the University of Washington campus, he was named Pro Player of the Year by *Sport* magazine in 1952.

8   Name the two head coaches in 1978 who brought the Forty Niners a 2–14 record.

9   In Super Bowl XVI, Ray Wersching tied the record for most field goals completed in the championship game. How many did he kick?

10   Name the player who picked up a fumble and ran sixty-six yards in the wrong direction to score a safety for the Niners.

MORE FORTY NINER FEVER

1   Frankie Albert.

2   R. C. Owens. The play got its name because Owens, a former basketball star, would leap in the air away from defenders.

3   Paul Hofer, named recipient of the Len Eshmont Award that year.

4   Howard Hickey introduced the formation in 1960 when the Forty Niners played Baltimore.

5   John Brodie.

6   The Chicago Bears. The final score was San Francisco 21, Chicago 17.

7   Hugh McElhenny.

8   Pete McCulley (1–8) was replaced by Fred O'Connor (1–6).

9   Four. Wersching became the Forty Niners' all-time leading scorer in 1985 with 789 points.

10   Minnesota Viking Jim Marshall. He made the play on October 25, 1964.

WHAT'S SILVER AND BLACK
AND AIN'T COMING BACK?
The Raiders

1   Where did the Oakland Raiders play their first game?

2   In 1972, Daryle Lamonica was the first starting quarterback and George Blanda was the second-string quarterback. Name the third-string quarterback for the Raiders.

3   *Scholastic Coach* magazine said he had "the most inventive mind in this country." Name the Raiders coach the magazine was praising.

4   Who were the Oakland Senors?

5   This Raiders quarterback was traded to Buffalo for Daryle Lamonica.

6   What team defeated the Raiders in Super Bowl II?

7   A graduate of the University of Santa Clara, he replaced Ken Stabler as quarterback in 1980.

8   He was named MVP in Super Bowl XI.

9   Name the two Raiders who wore jersey #16.

10   Give the final scores for Super Bowls XI and XV.

WHAT'S SILVER AND BLACK
AND AIN'T COMING BACK?
The Raiders

1   Kezar Stadium in 1960. They lost the game to the Dallas Texans.

2   Ken Stabler.

3   Al Davis, who became Raiders head coach in 1963.

4   The Raiders. Their original nickname was the Senors.

5   Tom Flores. He was Oakland's first quarterback in 1960.

6   Green Bay by a score of 33 to 14.

7   Dan Pastorini.

8   Fred Biletnikoff. He had played for Oakland when they lost to
Green Bay in Super Bowl II.

9   George Blanda and Jim Plunkett.

10 Super Bowl XI: Oakland 32, Minnesota 14; Super Bowl XV:
Oakland 27, Philadelphia 10.

THE AMAZING A's

1   This pitcher, signed by the A's in 1964, never pitched in the minor leagues.

2   Who said: "I am not trying to be popular. I am trying to make my team and my game popular."?

3   In what three consecutive years did the Oakland A's win the World Series?

4   Voted MVP in 1971, this player is a switch-hitter.

5   This future Hall of Famer played his final season with the A's in 1984.

6   Name the infielder who was suspended during the 1973 World Series for the errors he made during the game.

7   In his first World Series appearance, this catcher homered his first two times up to bat.

8   Another baseball first. In 1975, four A's pitchers combined to pitch a no-hitter. Who were they?

9   When Roy Eisenhardt fired A's manager Steve Boros in 1984, who replaced Boros?

10   What Berkeley native and former A's manager played in four World Series?

THE AMAZING A's

1 Jim "Catfish" Hunter, who was skilled at all sports in high school. Charlie Finley personally recruited Hunter from Jim's farm in Hertford, North Carolina, and put him in the major leagues.

2 Charlie O. Finley, former owner of the A's. Once an insurance salesman, Finley proposed many innovations that he thought would improve the game of baseball. Some of his ideas were night games for the World Series, brightly colored uniforms, orange baseballs, a three-ball walk and a two-strike strikeout, designated hitter, designated runner, a mechanical rabbit to provide baseballs, and bat girls.

3 1972, 1973 and 1974.

4 Vida Blue.

5 Joe Morgan.

6 Mike Andrews. Charlie Finley tried to get Andrews to sign a falsified medical report saying he was unfit to play.

7 Gene Tenace. In the 1972 series, he hit a total of four home runs to tie Babe Ruth's record.

8 Vida Blue, Paul Lindblad, Rollie Fingers and Glenn Abbott.

9 Jackie Moore.

10 Billy Martin played with the New York Yankees in the 1952, 1953, 1955 and 1956 World Series.

HOW 'BOUT THEM GIANTS

1   In 1984, one week after he was fired by the Giants, coach Frank Robinson had a new job. What was it?

2   This Giants player is well remembered for hitting Dodger player John Roseboro on the head with a bat.

3   In 1969, he was named Most Valuable Player in the All-Star Game.

4   On May 31, 1964, the San Francisco Giants and the New York Mets made the record books. How?

5   This manager was known for his controversial plus-and-minus system to evaluate players.

6   What three brothers all played in the Giants outfield at the same time?

7   Name the only San Francisco Giants pitcher to hit two home runs in one game.

8   This was the year the San Francisco Giants had their best win–loss record.

9   In 1973, this player led the Giants in home runs. He also pitched nine innings that season.

10 He was the Cy Young Award winner in 1967.

HOW 'BOUT THEM GIANTS

1   Batting coach for the Milwaukee Brewers.

2   Juan Marichal, who claimed that Roseboro made some unkind remarks about his mother.

3   Willie McCovey.

4   They played the longest game in baseball history: seven hours and twenty-three minutes. The Giants won 8 to 6.

5   Alvin Dark.

6   Jesus, Mateo (Matty) and Felipe Alou.

7   Jim Gott on May 12, 1985, playing against the St. Louis Cardinals. The Giants won 5 to 4 in the tenth inning.

8   The Giants' best win-loss year was 1962 (103–62), the same year they won the pennant.

9   Dave Kingman drove in twenty-four home runs that season.

10 Mike McCormick, who gave the best all-around performance as a pitcher in 1967.

GIANTS II

1   He holds the major league record for consecutive innings pitched, 269.1, without allowing a home run.

2   His uniform #24 was officially retired on August 20, 1983.

3   On June 21, 1976, the Giants made a triple play, Evans to Speier to Evans. What former Giant was at bat?

4   In 1982, he was the National League Comeback Player of the Year.

5   He had two hundred hits in the 1970 season.

6   Which Giants player won the gold glove in 1962 from the *Sporting News* All-Star Fielding Team?

7   Name three of the Giants who have had their uniform numbers retired.

8   In 1958, this Giants won the Rookie of the Year Award.

9   Name the Giants shortstop who was traded to Cleveland in May, 1985.

10   In 1963, 1966, 1968, 1969 and 1971 these three players were selected to play in the All-Star Game for the Giants.

GIANTS II

1   Greg Minton. The streak lasted from September 6, 1978, until May 2, 1982.

2   Willie Mays.

3   Willie McCovey. He was playing for the San Diego Padres.

4   Joe Morgan.

5   Bobby Bonds. Only one other Giant had more hits in a season: Willie Mays had 208 in 1958.

6   Jim Davenport.

7   Bill Terry, #3; Mel Ott, #4; Carl Hubbell, #11; Willie Mays, #24; Juan Marichal, #27; and Willie McCovey, #44.

8   Orlando Cepeda.

9   Johnnie LeMaster.

10   Juan Marichal, Willie McCovey and Willie Mays.

HOLY TOLEDO!
The Warriors

1   Who replaced Nate Thurmond as team captain of the Warriors in the 1974–75 season?

2   Surprisingly, he retired from basketball in 1981, while the Warriors were in contention for the playoffs.

3   Besides being the owner of the Warriors, Franklin Mieuli had a stake in what other professional sports teams?

4   His jersey #42 was retired in 1978.

5   Name the player whose eleven-year playing career stands as a Warrior record.

6   When the Warriors won the NBA Western Division championship in 1967, who was the head coach?

7   In the 1962–63 season, the Warriors' first in San Francisco, this player led the NBA in scoring.

8   In what year did the San Francisco Warriors move to Oakland?

9   At age fifty-eight, he was the oldest rookie coach in NBA history.

10   In what year were the Warriors world champions?

HOLY TOLEDO!
The Warriors

1   Rick Barry.

2   Center Clifford Ray quit the team with only two games to go. The Warriors lost both games and missed the playoffs.

3   In 1954, he purchased 10 percent of the Forty Niners and in 1958 he bought a share in the Giants.

4   Nate Thurmond.

5   Alvin Attles played from 1960 to 1971 and became the Warriors' general manager in 1983.

6   Bill Sharman.

7   Wilt "The Stilt" Chamberlain. He averaged an incredible 44.8 points a game.

8   In 1971. They changed their name to the Golden State Warriors.

9   John Bach, named head coach in 1983.

10   In 1975, when the Warriors swept the championship series in four straight games over the Washington Bullets.

GIVE 'EM THE AXE, THE AXE, THE AXE
College Sports

1   Name the former Cal quarterback who has played in the Super Bowl for two different teams.

2   Name the four Cal football players who lateralled the ball five times to defeat Stanford in the 1982 Big Game.

3   Name the Stanford basketball forward who was the national collegiate Player of the Year in 1937 with 17.1 points per game.

4   In 1951, this football team was undefeated in eleven games, but was *not* invited to a bowl game.

5   Name the Cal football coach who was undefeated and untied in the 1948 and 1949 seasons.

6   He was director of sports information at USF from 1950 to 1952.

7   Who were the "Vow Boys"?

8   Before becoming an NFL quarterback, he played for the New York Yankees' minor league team.

9   In the 1985 season, three former USF players were active in the NBA. Name them.

10 Who was Cal's quarterback in the 1959 Rose Bowl?

GIVE 'EM THE AXE, THE AXE, THE AXE
College Sports

1   Craig Morton played for the Cowboys and the Broncos in the Super Bowl.

2   Kevin Moen to Richard Rodgers to Dwight Garner (to Rodgers again) to Mariet Ford (to Moen again who ran through the Stanford band to score after time expired).

3   Angelo "Hank" Luisetti, a graduate of Galileo High School.

4   USF. Nine of the eleven players on that team went on to play in the NFL.

5   Lynn "Pappy" Waldorf. His only loss in those two years was to Northwestern in the Rose Bowl.

6   Pete Rozelle, who later went on to become the commissioner of the National Football League.

7   The Stanford freshman football team in 1933 vowed that they would never lose to USC and they never did.

8   Former Stanford quarterback John Elway.

9   Wallace Bryant (Dallas), Bill Cartwright (New York) and Quinton Dailey (Chicago).

10 Joe Kapp, who later went on to become head coach for Cal in 1982.

COLLEGE SPORTS II

1   This USF player won an Olympic gold medal for basketball in 1956.

2   This Bay Area school played Washington & Jefferson to a scoreless tie in a bowl game.

3   They are the only two players from the same college to be inducted into the NFL Hall of Fame in the same year.

4   They were the first father and son in history to put the shot over sixty feet.

5   This Cal runner was disqualified from the 1972 Olympic 100-meter dash semifinals.

6   Name the player who is the all-time basketball high scorer for USF.

7   Cal has three alumni who were quarterbacks active in the NFL in 1984. Name them.

8   This Stanford coach brought the T formation back to football.

9   Name the Cal player who ran sixty-five yards in the wrong direction during a Rose Bowl game.

10   What Stanford alumnus scored a NFL record of forty points in one game?

COLLEGE SPORTS II

1   Bill Russell.

2   Cal, in the 1922 Rose Bowl.

3   USF's Gino Marchetti and Ollie Matson.

4   Cal's Dave Maggard, Sr. (67 feet, 4.5 inches in 1968) and Dave Maggard, Jr. (60 feet, 3.25 inches in 1985).

5   Eddie Hart. Eddie was disqualified because he failed to show up for the event. His coach had misinformed him as to the time the event was to take place.

6   Forward Mary Hile (class of 1981) scored 2,324 points, followed by Bill Cartwright with 2,116 points. Hile's number (15) has been retired by USF, as well as those of Cartwright, Bill Russell and K. C. Jones.

7   Steve Bartkowski (the Falcons), Vince Ferragamo (the Rams) and Rich Campbell (the Packers).

8   Clark Shaughnessy in 1940.

9   Roy Riegels in 1929. He recovered a Georgia Tech fumble and headed for the goal line. Unfortunately he headed in the wrong direction; a teammate brought him down on the one-yard line.

10   Ernie Nevers scored six touchdowns and four extra points for the Chicago Cardinals, when they defeated the Chicago Bears on Thanksgiving Day, 1939.

STILL MORE COLLEGE SPORTS

1   What former USF basketball player went on to play football in the NFL?

2   This Cal sophomore set a record in the 100- and 200-meter butterfly in the 1984 Olympics.

3   Stanford played Michigan in the first Rose Bowl in 1902. In what year did Cal first play in Pasadena?
        a) 1921.   b) 1946.   c) 1903.   d) 1932.

4   This former Stanford running back was the first person to win the Olympic decathlon twice.

5   Name the Stanford sophomore who won one gold and two silver medals for swimming in the 1984 Olympic Games.

6   He was captain of USF's undefeated football team in 1951.

7   Name the Cal runner who broke the 400-meter world record in the 1936 Olympics.

8   What San Francisco State track star signed a recording contract with Columbia Records while preparing for the 1956 Olympics?

9   Cal won the national championship in this sport in 1973, 1974, 1975, 1977, 1983 and 1984.

10   This Mission High School graduate is the only woman in the City College of San Francisco Hall of Fame.

STILL MORE COLLEGE SPORTS

1   Ken McAllister, who played for the Kansas City Chiefs.

2   Mary T. Meagher, who was named Collegiate Female Athlete of the Year.

3   1921. The Bears defeated Ohio State 28–0.

4   Bob Mathias.

5   Pablo Morales.

6   Gino Marchetti.

7   Archie Moore.

8   Johnny Mathis. His high jump mark of 6 feet, 5.5 inches was a San Francisco State record for nine years.

9   Water polo.

10   Helen Crlenkovich. She was the women's national champion of both the three-meter board and platform diving in 1941 and 1945.

INDEX

210

215

ABOUT THE AUTHORS

A San Franciscan by choice, Karen Warner has lived in the Bay Area for
twelve years. When not writing trivia books, Karen is a humor
consultant to business executives. A cofounder of Golden Gate Writers,
she provides humorous material and writes pithy speeches for many of
the country's top CEOs.

Bill Dolon's first contact with Bay Area publishing was delivering phone
directories to Black Panther headquarters in 1971. Since then, he has
been a tour guide, a Bohemian Grove valet, a ghost-writer and a public
relations specialist. This is his first book.